NIGEL SLATER'S
REAL FOOD

NIGEL SLATER'S
REAL FOOD

Photographs by Jonathan Lovekin

FOURTH ESTATE · LONDON

For Louise Haines and Frances Whitaker

. . . and to the three of you with love

The author and publishers would like to thank the following for permission to include these recipes:

Page 92, Basic Roast Chicken; page 123, Chorizo with Potato (Spanish Stew); page 188, Hot Mushroom Sandwich; page 290, Sticky Chocolate Pudding – *How to Eat* by Nigella Lawson, Chatto & Windus, 1998. Page 71, Chicken, Buckwheat Noodle, Garlic and Coriander Laksa; page 249, Tamarind Ice-Cream – *The Sugar Club Cookbook*, Hodder, 1997. Page 124, Salsicce e Peperoni – *Alastair Little's Italian Kitchen*, Ebury, 1996. Pages 110–111, Matthew Fort on the cooking of sausages – *The Sausage Directory*, edited by Matthew Fort, Fourth Estate, 1992.

First published in Great Britain in 1998 by
Fourth Estate Limited, 6 Salem Road, London W2 4BU

Text © Nigel Slater 1998
Photographs © Jonathan Lovekin 1998

3 5 7 9 10 8 6 4 2

A catalogue record for this book is available from the British Library

ISBN 1-85702-971-2

Designed by Vivid Design

Colour Separations by Radstock Reproductions Ltd, Midsomer Norton
Printed in Great Britain by Butler and Tanner Ltd, Frome

'When I say butter, I mean unsalted; when I say salt, I mean Maldon sea salt; and, when I say sugar, I mean the golden unrefined stuff from Mauritius. Pepper is ground from a mill as I need it and not, absolutely not, bought ready-ground. Oh, and when I refer to a grill pan, I mean one of those heavy ridged, cast-iron grill pans that sits on the hob. You can now get them quite easily from cookware shops and department stores.'

CONTENTS

Thanks to: Elsa Acton Bond Tim Anderson Neil Arthur Michael Asare Tom Bancroft Jonathan Barker Adrian Barling Vicky Barnsley Robert Breckman Susie Burgin Tamsin Burnett-Hall Channel 4 Julian Clinkard Chantal Coady Nell Cooke-Hurle John Couzens Paul Cripps Susie Dunlop Lucy Eagle Nicky Eaton David Evans Matthew Fort Ben Frow Stephen Garrett John Gilbert Chris Godfrey Peter Gordon Emily Green Miles Green Louise Haines Trevor Hampton Paul Heathcote Victoria Heyworth-Dunne Kathryn Holliday Vanessa Kearns James Kellow Nigella Lawson Rowley Leigh Alastair Little Jonathan Lovekin Jill Martin Clova McCallum Sil McIlveen Richard McKerrow Aggie MacKenzie Patricia Michelson Jane Middleton Monica Murphy Colin Napthine Gavin Ogden Stephen Page Richard Partin Justine Picardie Chris Phinikas Simon Pinkerton Pont de La Tour Nicola Porter Christopher Potter Andrew Purvis Sarah Randell Peter and Suzanne Redstone Dominic Roberts Dean Simpole-Clark Rosemary Scoular Marella Shearer Kirsten Spiers Robin Sutherland Karen Taylor Tracey and Chris at Vivid Simon Walton Liz Warner Ruth Watson Frances Whitaker Neale Whitaker Araminta Whitley Sally Woodward Gentle Delia and Michael

REAL FOOD

By *Real Food* I mean big-flavoured, unpretentious cooking. Good ingredients made into something worth eating. Nothing fancy. Nothing extravagant. Nothing careless or slapdash. Just nice, uncomplicated food – be it chicken roasted with olive oil, lemon and basil or simply a big, fat mushroom baked in garlic butter and stuffed inside a soft bap. Simple food cooked with care and generosity.

This book is a collection of such food. More than a hundred recipes for the sort of stuff you can make for friends or family you want to have a good time with. This isn't show-off cooking designed to impress, the sort that uses every pot, pan, knife and sieve in the kitchen. This is nourishing, comforting food for those who like to eat for pleasure. Food for those who are prepared to take just a little care and effort to produce something really worthwhile. But neither is it the sort of food you have to fuss over.

There is nothing beyond the capabilites of even the most confirmed non-cook. Some recipes take ten minutes, others a couple of hours of slow, hands-off cooking. The only criterion is that they taste absolutely delicious. None is a wild and original combination. Instead they are about ingredients that quietly get along together, ingredients that 'feel right' together. (But that doesn't mean we can't have a bit of fun now and again.)

I remain convinced that some flavours and textures work perfectly together, that there are some ingredients that are, how shall I put it, meant for one another. Nothing will get me to believe in outlandish partnerships of ingredients brought together for the sake of originality. Some things are beyond the meddling of cookery writers and chefs. I think far too much is made of originality in cooking. No one will convince me that originality and good eating always go hand in hand.

This is not to say that cooking should stand still, but I see no point in bringing together flavours and textures that do not have something to offer one another. I don't care whether it is something as straightforward as the combination of crisp-crusted bread and ripe, oozing cheese, a slice of salty, aromatic ham and a juicy fig, good vanilla ice-cream and bitter chocolate sauce or something more complex such as the myriad textures and flavours in a plate of, say, roast pork and apple sauce – scrunchy crackling, hot velvety fat, savoury meat, unctuous gravy, tart sauce, sticky potatoes … I could go on.

Far better than coming over all inventive, I think, is to find an idea that you like, and work at it until it can be no better. What I would like to think I am doing with my recipes is to go most of the way for you, so that you can add, tweak and fiddle until you find something that is perfect for you. You may work a recipe of mine through and think that it needs a splash of cream, a shake of soy sauce or a squirt of lemon. Fine, I am happy with that. I like the recipes the way they are, and so do my testers, friends and colleagues. But that does not mean that I believe a recipe is a set of rules to be followed slavishly, as if they were carved in stone. There are too many variables for that, and one of those variables is your own taste.

I have brought a few friends' recipes along with me too. These are people whose approach to cooking I particularly admire and who are on the same 'wavelength'. They include: Nigella Lawson, *Vogue*'s foodwriter and author of *How To Eat*, Alastair Little and Rowley Leigh, who have been cooking some of London's most consistently delicious food for over a decade; and New

Zealander Peter Gordon who has brought the best of Pacific Rim cooking with him to London. I have also managed to get Emily Green of the *New Statesman* to guide me through making a perfect sandwich loaf, and Matthew Fort of the *Guardian* to let me into the secret of how to cook the perfect sausage.

In most cases the ingredients are as important as the cook or their recipe. There is a huge difference between cheap ice-cream that is made with vegetable fat and beet sugar and an ice-cream such as that made at Rocombe Farm, with organic cream and eggs, unrefined sugar and natural vanilla. Likewise the difference between a proper butcher's banger made from free-range pork and a sad little skinless supermarket sausage made from intensely-reared pigs.

Yes, of course, good food costs more, but would you rather have two robustly flavoured, sticky sausages than four thin, pink digits?

For this book, and for the television series of the same name, I have taken eight of my favourite foods; eight things about which I am truly passionate and produced a set of recipes in which they are especially good, and that I think are worth passing on to you. They are chicken, potatoes, garlic, sausages, bread, ice-cream and chocolate. So passionate am I about good bread that space and time has decreed I confine my recipes to those for sandwiches. But God, what sandwiches! Good ingredients simply prepared and served without ostentation. That's what I call real food. Be it a baked potato filled with cream, mustard and smoked haddock; a roast duck stuffed with potatoes to soak up its glorious cooking juices, or a bacon butty.

POTATOES

'If there is anything
better to eat than a plate
of hot, salty chips with a
bottle of ice-cold beer,
I have never found it.'

POTATO SUPPERS

Potato and Smoked Mackerel Dauphinoise
Stove-Top Dauphinoise with Pancetta and Rocket
Potato Pizza
Slow-Fried Potatoes with Thyme and Taleggio
Roast Duck with Marsala Gravy and Potato Stuffing
Mushroom and Potato Pie
Aromatic Pork Ribs with Melting Potatoes

CHIPS

Chips
Chips with Aïoli
Chips and Béarnaise
Chips and Roast Chilli Sauce
The Chip Butty

SPUDS ON THE SIDE

Best-Ever Mash
Parsley and Mustard Mash
Cheese Mash
Double Cheese Mash
Peter Gordon's Sweet Potato, Rosemary
and Garlic Mash
Roast Potatoes
Celeriac and Potato Cake

THE BAKED POTATO

The Perfect Baked Potato
Baked Potatoes with Basil and Parmesan
Baked Potatoes with Pancetta and Gorgonzola
Crushed Potatoes with Roast Tomatoes and Balsamic Vinegar
Baked Potatoes with Smoked Haddock and Mustard

POTATO SALAD

Warm Potato, Spinach and Parmesan Salad
Hot Fish and Chip Salad
Roast New Potato Salad
Classic French Potato Salad

THE HOT POTATO –
THE CULINARY EQUIVALENT
OF A BIG FAT HUG

What is it about eating a hot potato that makes me feel so good? Yes, of course, it is the most comforting and sustaining food of all, not to mention cheap and easy to come by, but there has to be more to it than that. Is it that when rubbed with salt and baked in the oven a plump potato warms me like nothing else? Could it be the way its flesh soaks up cream and garlic in a gratin, or mashes so blissfully with butter? Might it be the way its outside crisps and shines when roasted round the Sunday joint while its inside stays moist and gooey?

Perhaps it is the pleasure I get from squashing a naked, virginal steamed potato into the gravy of a lamb casserole, or that moment when the creamed potato topping of a shepherd's pie – at first crisp and furrowed, then underneath smooth and soothing – hits my tongue. Maybe it is hearing the salty rustle of the thinnest *frites* round a sizzling and bloody steak. Or could it be that second when I smash open a baked potato with my fist (the only way to ensure a *truly* fluffy spud) and its solid white flesh turns to hot snow?

Or could it just be that the texture of a baked, fried, creamed or roast potato is the one thing that continues to comfort, soothe and reassure me in such a mad, hostile and unpredictable world?

A Question of Texture ...

Not enough is said about the texture of food. In my book it goes hand in hand with flavour, combining to make something that is either good to eat or it isn't. And so it is with spuds. Sometimes we want a dry, fluffy potato that crisps up well – for baking or roasting, for instance – and other times we want something smooth and slippery for a salad or gratin. The texture of a cooked potato is generally either waxy or floury. Waxy potatoes usually have creamy-yellow flesh – all dense and fudgy – and contain less starch than floury ones. They are particularly suitable for salads as they tend not to break up when they absorb the dressing. Likewise in a gratin, the slices staying whole whilst soaking up the garlic-scented cream. Their skins are thin and rarely need removing – although if you do you will end up with the most beautiful, long, shiny, elegant potatoes imaginable.

Waxy potatoes are often sold under the name of salad potatoes. Something of an understatement when you think how fine they also are when simply boiled or steamed. Some people use them for mash, in which case you get a sublimely gooey purée that for some reason tastes better in restaurants than it does at home. The easiest-to-find varieties are the long, pink-skinned Pink Fir Apple, Charlotte, La Ratte and Belle de Fontenay.

Floury potatoes have much coarser flesh – they are higher in starch – and tend to crumble easily when boiled or roasted. They produce a drier purée when mashed. This dry, mealy flesh means they have a tendency to break up. This can be a good thing when you are frying up yesterday's boiled potatoes in a pan, the slices crumbling enticingly as they turn golden and faintly crisp in the hot butter.

Famous floury tatties are King Edward, red-skinned Romano and the lovely Maris Piper. They make an old-fashioned mash that will stand in fluffy peaks firm enough to stick your sausage in. Yet, having said this, I have had wonderful mash made with the yellowest waxy spuds and I rather like it when floury Edwards dissolve into the garlicky cream of a slow-baked gratin.

POTATO AND SMOKED MACKEREL DAUPHINOISE

You might need some salad leaves such as rocket or baby spinach to wipe up the mustardy, smoky cream from your plate. Or perhaps some green beans.

Serves 4 as a main dish

450g waxy potatoes, scraped
225g smoked mackerel fillets
2 bay leaves
300ml double cream
200ml full cream milk
1 tablespoon grain mustard

Slice the potatoes lengthways, about as thick as one-pound coins. Put them in a shallow baking dish about 30cm in diameter. Break the mackerel fillets into large, bite-sized pieces and toss them gently with the potatoes. Try not to break the fish up too much. Tuck in the bay leaves.

Mix together the cream, milk, mustard and a little salt and pepper, then pour it over the potatoes. Bake in an oven preheated to 190°C/Gas 5 for about one hour, till the cream is bubbling and the potatoes are knife-tender.

STOVE-TOP DAUPHINOISE WITH PANCETTA AND ROCKET

Serves 4 as a light lunch or 3 as a more substantial main dish

2 tablespoons olive oil
2 plump cloves of garlic, peeled and crushed
100g pancetta, diced
1kg waxy potatoes, scraped and thinly sliced
100g rocket
200ml double cream
100ml full cream milk
50g Parmesan, grated

Warm the olive oil in a large, high-sided frying or sauté pan over a moderate heat. When it starts to bubble, add the garlic and pancetta and cook slowly so that the fat melts into the oil. Add the potato slices and let them cook, still over a moderate heat, so that they soak up some of the fat from the pancetta. This will add to the flavour and give them a velvety texture.

After fifteen minutes or so they will have softened and started to colour here and there (do not worry if they crumble a little). Roughly chop the rocket and add to the potatoes. Mix the cream and milk together and pour over. Season with salt and pepper and bring very slowly to the boil.

When the liquid in the pan starts to bubble, turn down the heat and cover with a lid. The heat should be very low, so that the cream does not burn on the bottom of the pan. Leave to simmer for ten minutes, until the potatoes are starting to absorb the cream. Scatter over the Parmesan and stir lightly in. Continue cooking until the cheese has melted – a matter of a couple of minutes – then serve.

POTATO PIZZA

Makes 2

180g waxy potatoes
a medium-sized onion, peeled and thinly sliced
4 tablespoons olive oil
a small palmful of thyme leaves
120g taleggio or fontina cheese
4 tablespoons crème fraîche
more olive oil and shavings of Parmesan

For the base:
3 level tablespoons wholemeal flour
225g plain flour
$\frac{1}{2}$ teaspoon salt
7g sachet of easy-blend dried yeast
a tablespoon of milk
2 tablespoons olive oil

For the base, mix the flours together in a large bowl, then add the salt, yeast, milk, olive oil and 120ml warm water (adding more water or flour if necessary) to give a firm dough. Knead on a flat surface for ten minutes. If you have a mixer with a dough hook, use that instead. Set aside for thirty minutes in an oiled bowl.

Slice the potatoes thinly and bring them to the boil in salted water, then turn down to a simmer for five minutes. Drain thoroughly. Fry the onion in the oil till soft.

Put a large baking sheet in an oven preheated to 220°C/Gas 7 to heat up. Turn the dough out, flatten it and cut it in half. Press each piece with your fist into a round roughly 23cm in diameter. Leave to rise in a warm place for five to ten minutes.

Divide the onion, potatoes, thyme, cheese and crème fraîche between the bases. Slide the pizzas on to the heated baking sheet, drizzle with a little more oil and scatter with shavings of Parmesan, then bake for twenty minutes, till the bases are crisp.

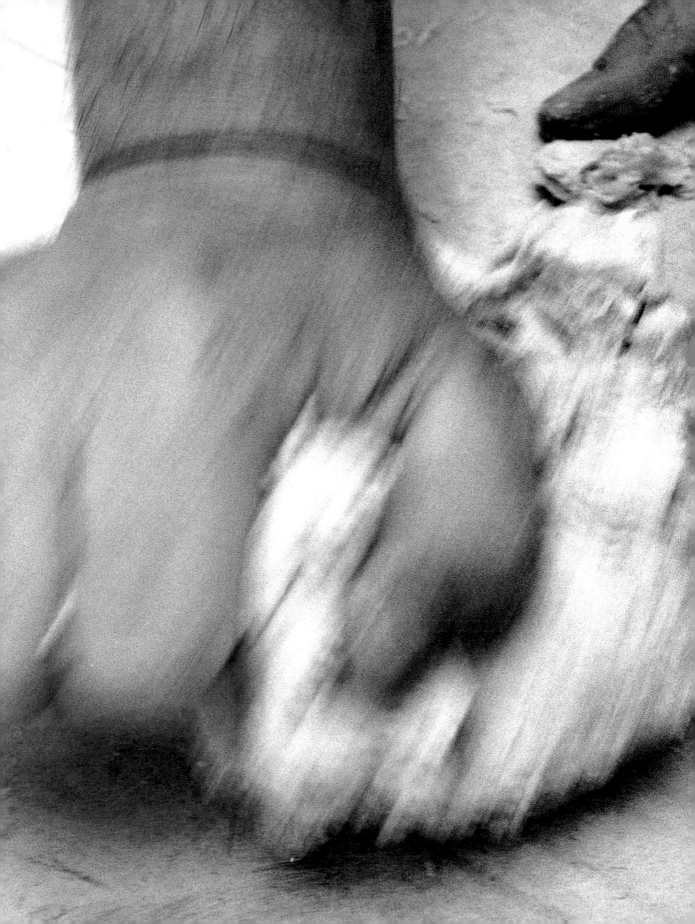

Slow-Fried Potatoes with Thyme and Taleggio

When I say waxy potatoes, I mean the yellow-fleshed varieties such as Charlotte and Belle de Fontenay. Supermarkets often label them 'salad potatoes'. They keep their buttery texture, and shape, when baked slowly in cream or stock.

Serves 2 as a main course or 4 as a side dish for, say, grilled ham or
    cold chicken

500g waxy potatoes
a medium onion, peeled and thinly sliced
2 tablespoons olive oil
50g (a thick slice) butter
2 cloves of garlic, peeled and sliced
a small palmful of thyme leaves
100g semi-soft cheese such as taleggio or fontina

Slice the potatoes into rounds the thickness of pound coins. Fry the sliced onion gently in the oil and butter in a shallow pan about 22cm in diameter. As it becomes soft and pale gold add the potatoes, a little salt and ground pepper, the garlic and thyme and toss gently to coat the spuds in oil and herbs.

Turn the heat as low as possible and cover the pan so that the potatoes cook slowly, stirring them from time to time. After forty to fifty minutes they will be soft and golden. Slice the cheese thinly, lay it on the potatoes and cover the pan again. It will have melted after a couple of minutes.

ROAST DUCK WITH MARSALA GRAVY AND POTATO STUFFING

I like my roast duck properly cooked and with crisp skin – none of that pink-fleshed lukewarm duck for me, thank you. In this recipe much of the fat and juices that run from the duck as it roasts are soaked up by the crushed potatoes inside. My suggestion of serving roast potatoes too is partly to provide a crisp contrast to the gloriously moist spuds in the stuffing and partly pure greed.

Serves 2 generously

a plump duck, about 2kg
750g floury potatoes, peeled and cut for boiling
2 medium onions, peeled and thinly sliced
50g butter
a bushy sprig of rosemary
4 bay leaves
a wine glass of Marsala, plus a little extra
a very little flour
a ladleful of stock or water

Prick the duck all over with a meat fork, then put the bird in the sink and pour a kettle of boiling water over it. If you have time to do this once or even twice more, all the better. Put the duck somewhere cool (not the fridge) for an hour or more, during which time the skin will dry out. This is the classic Chinese way to ensure crisp skin.

Boil the potatoes till almost tender. Meanwhile, cook the onions in the butter in a frying pan till golden and soft. Drain the potatoes, set half of them aside and crush the rest roughly with a fork. Mix the crushed ones with the cooked onions and some salt and pepper.

Put the duck in a roasting tin, surrounded by the reserved boiled potatoes. Fill the inside of the duck with the crushed potatoes and onions, the whole stem of rosemary and the bay. Rub a little salt over the skin, then roast the duck in an oven preheated to 200°C/Gas 6 for thirty minutes. Baste the roasting potatoes with any fat that is coming from the duck. Pour the Marsala into the roasting tin. Continue to roast for forty to forty-five minutes, until the skin is crisp and the flesh brown (not pink) and moist.

Lift the duck and potatoes out and leave to rest. Pour most of the fat into a basin (you can roast potatoes in it later in the week), leaving any juices underneath behind in the tin, then put the roasting tin over a moderate flame. Sprinkle over a tablespoon (no more) of flour and stir it round to cook and soak up the liquid in the pan. When it starts to colour, add a little more Marsala and a ladleful of stock or water. Let this bubble away and thicken – slightly – whilst you scrape at any gooey bits in the pan, stirring them in. Taste and season with salt and pepper.

Carve the duck and serve with the potato stuffing, roast potatoes and gravy.

Mushroom and Potato Pie

This is better described as garlic mushrooms and melting cheese in a Parmesan mashed potato crust. It will stand up for itself as a main dish but also works well as a side dish for cold roast meats.

Serves 4, with buttered spinach

1.5kg floury potatoes
50g butter
100ml hot milk
2 free range eggs, beaten
75g Parmesan, freshly grated

For the filling:
350g brown mushrooms
50g butter
2 cloves of garlic, peeled and sliced
2 tablespoons chopped parsley
200g fontina or Gruyère

Cook the potatoes in boiling salted water till tender, then peel them (their skins should just slip off) and mash with the butter and hot milk. Stir in the eggs and two-thirds of the Parmesan.

While the potatoes are cooking, cut the mushrooms into thick slices or quarters and fry them with the butter and garlic till golden and sweet. Season with the parsley and some salt and pepper. Lightly butter a 23cm cake tin or round baking dish.

Smooth half the mashed potato over the bottom of the dish, then cube the cheese and put it on top. Scatter the mushrooms and any cooking juices over the cheese and smooth the remaining mashed potato over them. Dust with the remaining Parmesan. Bake in an oven preheated to 190°C/Gas 5 for thirty minutes, till the crust is golden.

Aromatic Pork Ribs with Melting Potatoes

You can use Marsala in place of the Madeira. A chicory salad would be good afterwards.

Serves 4

6 medium-sized floury potatoes
4 bay leaves
the juice of a lemon
6 large cloves of garlic, peeled and crushed
a tablespoon of olive oil
$\frac{1}{2}$ teaspoon fennel seeds
a tablespoon of unrefined light brown sugar
a teaspoon of sea salt
4 tablespoons stock
4 tablespoons Madeira
a length of large, meaty, pork ribs about 1kg in weight, in the piece

Cut each potato into ten slices and put them in a lightly oiled roasting tin, tucking the bay leaves in here and there.

Mix together the lemon juice, garlic, olive oil, fennel seeds, sugar, sea salt and a heavy grinding of black pepper, then stir in the stock and Madeira. Put the pork ribs, still in the piece, on top of the potatoes and spread the seasoning mixture over the back and front of the meat. Cover the roasting tin with foil and bake in an oven preheated to 180°C/Gas 4 for an hour and a half, basting with the baking juices half-way through cooking.

Remove the foil and turn the heat up to 200°C/Gas 6, baste and return to the oven for a further fifty minutes, basting once. Finally, turn the oven up to 220°C/Gas 7, baste and roast for thirty minutes, till the meat is deep golden brown and the potatoes golden and melting. Remove the pork, but leave the potatoes in the switched-off oven, and leave the meat to rest for five minutes.

Cut the meat into thick slices, spooning over any juices left in the pan, and serve the spuds on the side.

CHIPS

What I want of a chip depends on my mood. A rustling pile of thin *frites* with a rare steak; a parcel of slightly soggy thick-cut chips soaked in rough vinegar on the way home from the pub; or something in between – crisp and thick and fluffy inside – for pigging out at home with hot chilli sauce or a pot of garlicky mayonnaise as a 'chip dip'. As much as I love elegant, white steamed potatoes, crunchy potato skins, or light-as-a-dream *pommes soufflées*, sometimes it just has to be chips.

The spuds should be of the big, floury variety – Maris Piper, Edwards – and need two fryings in clear, hot oil or dripping. The first to soften; the next, at a higher temperature, to crisp.

Enough for 2

4 large, floury potatoes
2 litres melted dripping or lard or sunflower oil for deep-frying

Peel the potatoes and cut them into long, thick slices, about as long and thick as your fingers. Unless you have very big hands, in which case you should aim for about 1cm in width. Leave them in cold water to stop them sticking together.

Put the fat or oil to heat in a deep pan over a low flame. Bring it slowly up to 150°C. If you don't have a kitchen thermometer, you can check by adding a chip to the oil – if it sinks, then the oil is not hot enough. If it floats in a mass of bubbles, the temperature is right. Drain the chips and dry them on a clean tea towel, then put them in a frying basket and lower them gently into the fat. They will crackle and bubble alarmingly. Let them fry for about five minutes, until they are soft but still pale. Lift out and drain. Bring the oil up to 185°C. Be very careful at this point – the fat is very dangerous (you know this, but I just want to remind you). Return the chips to the fat for three to four minutes, shaking the basket now and again to help them brown evenly.

When they are golden brown and crisp, drain briefly on kitchen paper. Salt them enthusiastically and please don't forget to turn off the fat.

CHIPS WITH AÏOLI

In an emergency, a jar of Hellman's will suffice. But only in an emergency.

Enough for 2

the chips as before
2 cloves of garlic, young and plump
2 large free range egg yolks
300ml fruity extra virgin olive oil

Peel the garlic and mash to a paste with about half a teaspoon of salt, using a pestle and mortar or a small, stiff whisk and a heavy bowl. Stir in the yolks with a grinding of pepper, then add the olive oil drop by drop, quickening to a trickle as the sauce thickens. Take it easy. You should end up with a bright yellowy-green mayonnaise that will stand in peaks.

Now dip your hot chips in that.

Chips and Béarnaise

The ideal accompaniment to this would be a thin, rare steak.

Like its blander, but equally delicious sister Hollandaise, Béarnaise sauce has a habit of splitting. If this happens, put a couple of egg yolks in a clean bowl over the hot water and slowly whisk in the curdled sauce.

Enough for 2 as a snack

the chips as before
3 tablespoons white wine vinegar
a shallot, peeled and chopped
6 black peppercorns
a teaspoon of dried tarragon
2 free range egg yolks
a teaspoon of Dijon mustard
150g soft, almost melted, butter
a palmful of chopped tarragon leaves

Bring the vinegar, shallot, peppercorns and dried tarragon to the boil with 2 tablespoons of water in a small pan. Simmer till there is almost no liquid left. We are only talking about a couple of minutes here.

Put the egg yolks in a heatproof bowl over a pan of simmering water. Working quickly, add the mustard, then whisk in the dregs of liquid from the small pan, leaving the solids behind. Now gently whisk in the butter a little at a time. Once the sauce has thickened, stir in the tarragon and a little salt. Keep whisking, slowly and regularly. It should be as thick as custard.

Pour into a warm bowl and eat with the chips.

Chips and Roast Chilli Sauce

Put the beers in the fridge, rent a video and make plenty of this.

Enough for 4

the chips as before
6 ripe tomatoes
3 hot red chillies
4 cloves of garlic
2 teaspoons soft brown sugar
2 teaspoons tomato purée
the juice of a lime
3 tablespoons extra virgin olive oil
3 tablespoons finely chopped coriander leaves

Roast the tomatoes, chillies and garlic in an oven preheated to 180°C/Gas 4 until the tomato skins are blackened. Squeeze the garlic from its skin. Whizz the tomatoes and chillies (including the skins) in a food processor with the garlic, brown sugar, tomato purée, lime juice, olive oil and coriander until they form a coarse pulp. Add salt to taste and set aside for several hours for the flavours to marry. Eat with the chips.

THE CHIP BUTTY

If you are making chips at home for a chip butty, then all I can say is
that you are a real hero. My need for this starch marathon is usually
confined to when I have had too much to drink and not enough to eat.
It is sod's law that not all pubs serving good beer also serve good food.
No amount of cheese and onion crisps will soak up a whole evening's
drink, which is when the butty comes into its own. Ideally you pick up
the chips on the way home, spread an absurdly generous amount of
butter on the bread, then pile on the chips. The crux of the matter is
the temperature of the chips, which must still be hot enough to melt
the butter. Salty, buttery fingers are an indescribably good feast when
you are a bit pissed. Especially when they are someone else's.

BEST-EVER MASH

This recipe is reprinted almost verbatim from my book *Real Cooking*. No matter what tweaks and changes I make, I still think it is the best mash recipe. And heaven knows, I have tried them all.

The mash I adore is the sort that is fluffy, yet rich with butter. There should be no lumps and it must stand in soft, creamy clouds, not slouch all over the plate like a ripe cheese. Much depends on the potato, which must be of the floury variety, such as King Edward or Maris Piper. You can make a nice mash with a yellow waxy potato but it is a different thing altogether, and temperamental, too. Leave it to the chefs who do it so beautifully. What we are after here is giant piles of blissful mash. The sort you want to bury your face in.

Serves 4

900g floury potatoes such as King Edwards, Maris Piper or Desirée
100g butter
100ml hot milk – not essential but gives a fluffier mash

Rinse the potatoes, put them in a large pan of cold water and bring up to the boil. Salt generously and partially cover with a lid. Simmer until the potatoes are tender to the point of a knife, then drain them. Pull off the skins – they should peel away easily. You can wear rubber gloves if you like, or struggle with an oven glove. I hold them in my hands as best I can and tell myself a little pain is good for me.

Throw the hot, peeled potatoes back into the pan and return them to the heat. Hold them briefly over the heat to dry off completely and become even fluffier. Mash them with the butter using a metal potato masher. There should be no lumps. Pour in the milk, which should be hot rather than boiling, and beat the mixture with a wooden spoon or Kenwood beater till it is fluffy and light. You might want to add more salt. One must work quickly if the mash is to be hot. And it must be hot, and buttery, gloriously buttery.

Parsley and Mustard Mash

Sometimes I like a lighter, fluffier version of this. Perhaps if I am eating it with fish rather than, say, sausages. In which case I beat the potatoes, butter and crème fraîche with one of those hand-held electric beaters till light and fluffy, then fold in the mustard and parsley.

Serves 2 generously

750g floury potatoes, peeled and cut into large chunks
50g butter
2 heaped tablespoons grain mustard
a handful of parsley leaves, roughly chopped
3 heaped tablespoons crème fraîche

Boil the potatoes in a deep pan of salted water till tender to the point of a knife. Drain and mash thoroughly with the butter, mustard, parsley and crème fraîche, using a potato masher. You are unlikely to need salt or pepper; the other seasonings are quite adequate. Cover with a butter paper and a tight lid and keep warm, if not eating immediately.

Cheese Mash

Now I have to admit I can cheerfully sit down in a squashy chair and eat an entire plateful of this while watching some unchallenging Hollywood film, but the idea really is to use it on the side with some grilled bacon rashers or perhaps grilled chicken.

Enough for 2

750g medium-sized floury potatoes
50g butter
300g Gruyère, fontina or gorgonzola, cubed

Cook the potatoes in boiling, salted water till tender to the point of a knife. Remove the skins and mash the flesh with the butter till fluffy. Immediately (i.e. while the potato is still very hot) throw in the cubed cheese and stir. Serve straight away, so that the cheese oozes in the heat of the spuds.

Double Cheese Mash

As above but scoop the whole lot into an ovenproof dish. Scatter with a handful of grated Parmesan and an equal amount of fine white breadcrumbs, then bake in a very hot oven till the top is golden and faintly crisp.

PETER GORDON'S SWEET POTATO, ROSEMARY AND GARLIC MASH

A light, fragrant and beautifully coloured mash from Peter Gordon.

Serves 4 as a side dish

1kg sweet potatoes, peeled and cut roughly into 2cm dice
200g unsalted butter
1 red chilli, finely sliced
2 cloves of garlic, peeled and finely sliced
2 dessertspoons fresh rosemary leaves, roughly chopped

Put the potatoes in a pan, cover with cold water, add a few teaspoons of salt and boil until tender, just like ordinary potatoes.

Meanwhile, heat up the butter in a small pan and, when melted, add the remaining ingredients. Cook over a moderate heat until the garlic begins to colour, stirring from time to time, then take off the heat.

Drain and mash the potatoes, then stir in the chilli mixture. Taste for seasoning and serve.

ROAST POTATOES

The difference between a good roast potato and a sublime roast potato depends on your willingness to put in a little bit of effort. The best roast spuds – by which I mean the crispest, gooiest, stickiest roast spuds – are those you take the trouble to give a quick boil in salted water before you roast them. After boiling and a gentle rough and tumble, the potatoes will soften just enough to fray and crush a little along the edges. When roasted in the hot fat, they will sport the rustling, crusty edges and melting interior that distance the sublime roast potato from the merely good one.

Serves 4

900g (about 5) large, floury potatoes, such as King Edward
fat from the roast or lard or dripping

Peel the potatoes and cut them into pieces large enough for you to have to take two bites at. Any smaller and they will be all crust and no spud. Put them in a saucepan of cold water and bring to the boil. Add salt, a teaspoon or so, and turn down to a frisky boil. Leave them cooking for five minutes, then drain them.

Take the pan in both hands and give it a couple of good shakes. The idea is to fluff the edges of the spuds up so that they become crisp and frilly as they roast. Tip them into the roasting tin in which you are roasting the joint. (If you are not roasting a joint, use a shallow metal tin in which you have heated enough lard, dripping or even olive oil to form a thin layer on the bottom.)

Roll the spuds in the fat, then roast in an oven preheated to 200°C/Gas 6 until thoroughly golden and crisp. A good forty-five minutes, maybe longer. Move them only once or twice during cooking, otherwise the edges will not crisp and brown. Tip off any extra fat, crumble sea salt over them and send them back to the oven for a few minutes till they are deep, golden brown.

Celeriac and Potato Cake

Celeriac is one of our most overlooked vegetables. Creamy green, round and bewhiskered, it is usually found near the parsnips and swedes. Its flavour – like mild, earthy celery – works well with potatoes.

This makes a fine side dish for cold roast beef, slices of Parma ham, grilled cod, haddock or mackerel. I have been known to eat it as a main course on its own.

Serves 4 as a side dish

500g waxy potatoes, peeled
a medium-sized celeriac, peeled
90g butter
4 cloves of garlic, peeled and thinly sliced
2 heaped tablespoons Dijon mustard
a level tablespoon of thyme leaves
60ml vegetable stock
a handful of dill leaves

Slice the potatoes and celeriac so thinly you can see through them. Mix them together and soak in cold water. Melt the butter in a metal-handled, deep frying pan (one that can go in the oven) and when it starts to bubble add the garlic and cook slowly for five minutes, till it is soft and has perfumed the butter.

Take off the heat and stir in the mustard, thyme leaves and a grinding of salt and pepper. Drain the potatoes and celeriac and dry them on kitchen paper. Toss them in the mustard butter so that they are wet all over, then loosely flatten them and pour in the stock. Cover with a circle of greaseproof paper, then bake in an oven preheated to 190°C/Gas 5 for an hour and ten minutes, until tender to the point of a knife.

Remove the greaseproof, turn up the heat to 220°C/Gas 7 and bake for a further ten minutes, until coloured and lightly crisp on top. Tear the dill up a bit and scatter it over the top and into the juices.

THE BAKED POTATO

Surely the perfect baked potato is crisp, salty and rough outside, all 'fluff and butter' within. My friend Rosie Stark told me to hit my baked spud with a neat karate blow instead of a knife as it comes from the oven. It guarantees a baked potato that is as light as snow inside. The accepted rule is to use a large, floury-textured variety such as Maris Piper or King Edward. For the classic cold-weather baked tatties, the sort that drips butter down your shirt, they are unbeatable.

But small, yellow-fleshed, waxy spuds can be baked too. They appeal most with tart, bright-flavoured accompaniments instead of butter or cheese. Roasted sweet-tart tomatoes, perhaps, or the juices from a roast chicken into which you have stuffed a lemon or two.

A baked potato is a humble feast until we get out the butter, the cheese, the olive oil, the gravy and the cream. But surely that is what a baked potato is for.

THE PERFECT BAKED POTATO

A baked potato loses some of its majesty if it isn't a big, fat one. So go for the biggest in the bag, give it a good wash and, while it is still damp, sprinkle it with crushed sea salt. Not quite as much salt as in the picture (I went a bit over the top). Now prick the skin here and there with a fork and bake on the bars of an oven preheated to about 200°C/Gas 6 for a good hour, maybe an hour and a quarter. The time will, of course, depend on the size and variety of your choice — whatever wait you are in for, it will seem interminable.

The potato is done when it gives to a little pressure from thumb and forefinger. It will also be singing quietly to itself. Its skin will crackle as you lift it hot and glorious from the oven.

Remove immediately and hit it with the side of your hand (wrapped in a tea towel if you would rather not burn yourself), hard enough to split the skin but not so hard that you re-decorate the kitchen. A plume of steam will leave the potato with a rush, leaving the inside a mass of light, powdery, moist fluff. This is where you get the butter out.

Allow a big one per person.

BAKED POTATOES WITH BASIL AND PARMESAN

Shop-bought pesto is a good second best (just remember that it *is* second best).

Enough for 2 as a light supper, perhaps with a leafy salad and
   pudding after

4 baked potatoes as before
3 plump cloves of garlic, peeled
2 large handfuls of basil leaves (about 15g)
2 tablespoons pine nuts, lightly toasted
4 tablespoons olive oil
2 tablespoons grated Parmesan, plus extra to finish

Cream the garlic to a paste with a little salt using a pestle and mortar. Add the basil and pine nuts, pounding to a thick paste. Drizzle in the oil, stirring, then mix in the Parmesan. You should have a bright green, deeply fragrant, sloppy paste.

Crack the baked potatoes open, scoop out the flesh and return the empty skins to the oven to crisp. Mash the potato and pesto together, then pile into the skins. Scatter with more grated cheese and bake till bubbling.

BAKED POTATOES WITH PANCETTA AND GORGONZOLA

If pancetta – the mild, aromatic Italian bacon – proves elusive, then you could use diced rashers of streaky instead.

Enough for 2 as a main dish with spinach salad

4 baked potatoes as before
100g pancetta, cubed
150g double cream
100g gorgonzola, diced

Fry the pancetta till its fat is golden, using a little butter or oil if necessary. Stir in the cream and gorgonzola and leave to bubble gently at a moderate heat for a minute or two.

Split the potatoes, then spoon in dollops of the smoky, creamy sauce.

CRUSHED POTATOES WITH ROAST TOMATOES AND BALSAMIC VINEGAR

Enough for 2 as a light main course

400g waxy potatoes
sea salt
500g cherry tomatoes
olive oil
2 teaspoons balsamic vinegar
a tablespoon of whole black peppercorns, coarsely ground

Rinse the potatoes and roll them lightly in sea salt. Bake them in an oven preheated to 200°C/Gas 6 till knife-tender – about forty minutes. Drizzle the tomatoes lightly with olive oil and a little salt, then roast for thirty minutes in a shallow tin.

When the tomatoes start to burst their skins they are ready. Crush the potatoes lightly with a heavy spoon or potato masher so they crack open, then spoon the tomatoes over and to the side, leaving the juices behind in the tin. Stir the balsamic vinegar into the juices with most of the black pepper, putting the rest of it in a little dish for anyone who wants more. Slosh the sweet, peppery juices over the potatoes.

Baked Potatoes with Smoked Haddock and Mustard

Serves 2 as a main course, with salad and a pudding

4 baked potatoes as before
225g smoked haddock
300ml double cream
2 tablespoons grain mustard
a palmful of parsley leaves, chopped

Put the smoked haddock in a shallow baking dish skin-side down. Season the cream with the mustard, parsley and a little salt and pepper and pour it over the haddock. Bake in the same oven as the potatoes until the flakes of the fish fall apart easily – about twenty minutes.

Break open the potatoes, scrape the flesh into a bowl, then return the empty skins to the oven to crisp a little if necessary. Mash the potato with the cream from the cooked fish, whipping it with a hand-held beater to get it smooth. Tease the flesh from the skin of the fish with a fork, keeping the flakes as whole as possible. Stir them into the creamed potato, check the seasoning, then pile back into the hot potato skins and place briefly under a hot grill until the peaks of potato start to crisp and colour.

POTATO SALAD

A punchy olive oil, mustard and vinegar dressing often seems more flattering to potatoes than one made with mayonnaise, resulting in a salad that tastes clean and bright. Don't get me wrong – a thoughtfully made potato mayonnaise can be good to eat too. It is just that it is so often made without care.

Small things matter, especially with something as simple as a potato salad. The right potato, properly cooked, a vibrant dressing, and enough time for the potato to soak it up are all it takes to lift the mundane into something worth eating.

Small, oval, yellow-fleshed potatoes work best in a salad because they keep their shape when they absorb the dressing. Their flesh is buttery when cooked. The surface of the potato feels waxy as you slice it. A floury potato will feel wet in the mouth and crumble as you toss it in the salad. Often labelled 'salad' potatoes, the easiest-to-find varieties of waxy spud are La Ratte, Charlotte, Belle de Fontenay and Pink Fir Apple. Once cooked, the skins slither off effortlessly. If they cling to the potato, then don't push it, just serve them as they are.

The trick is to dress the potatoes while they are still hot – a little thing that makes so much difference to the flavour of the finished salad. Forget the wet, white slush of commerce and cafeterias; a mindfully made *salade de pommes de terre*, carefully dressed with wine vinegar, olive oil and mustard, and seasoned with black pepper and chopped parsley, can be a joy to eat. Especially if the cook cares enough to have meticulously skinned the potatoes.

Warm Potato, Spinach and Parmesan Salad

This is one of the big, butch salads that taste much better than they look. A Saturday lunch sort of salad and, if you like, a side dish to a plate of cold chicken.

Serves 2 as a main-course salad

500g waxy potatoes
4 tablespoons balsamic vinegar
the juice of a lemon
2 heaped tablespoons Dijon mustard
12 tablespoons olive oil
a large lump of young Parmesan
8 rashers of streaky bacon
6 handfuls of small spinach leaves, washed

Lower the potatoes into boiling, salted water and cook over a moderate heat till tender – about ten to fifteen minutes. Drain and slice thickly.

Meanwhile, whizz the vinegar, lemon juice, mustard and olive oil in a blender or food processor with 4 heaped tablespoons of grated Parmesan. (If you mix by hand, whisk the vinegar, lemon juice and mustard together, then beat in the oil and cheese.) Grind in a little black pepper.

Fry or grill the rashers till crisp and golden. Drain on kitchen paper, then tear into small strips.

Put the spinach in a salad bowl, torn or shredded if you wish, add the warm potatoes and the bacon, then toss gently with the dressing. Leave for ten minutes before serving, scattering shavings of Parmesan over the salad as you go.

HOT FISH AND CHIP SALAD

I know this sounds a bit wacky but it is a really good dish – if a little
on the rustic side – with bags of flavour. Trust me.

Serves 4 as a main course

400g cod fillet, skinned
300g squid, cleaned and cut into thick rings
200g fine fresh breadcrumbs
400g small waxy potatoes
groundnut oil
3 bunches of watercress and 1 bunch of rocket

For the dressing:
a large bunch of flat-leafed parsley, stalks removed
6 bushy sprigs of mint, stalks removed
8 anchovy fillets, rinsed
2 cloves of garlic, crushed
a tablespoon of Dijon mustard
3 tablespoons capers, rinsed
6 tablespoons extra virgin olive oil
2 tablespoons lemon juice

Cut the cod into large pieces, about 5cm long. Roll the cod and squid in the crumbs. Halve the potatoes lengthways and lower them into boiling salted water for five minutes. Drain, then fry them gently in shallow oil till soft and golden – a matter of fifteen to twenty minutes – turning occasionally.

Whilst they cook, whizz the dressing ingredients briefly in a blender (or chop the herbs and anchovies, then beat in the other ingredients). You want a thick, lumpy, vivid green sludge.

Once the potatoes are done, remove them from the pan and drain on kitchen paper. Pour in more oil and, when it is really hot and sizzling, add the crumbed fish. Fry till golden, then drain on kitchen paper.

Divide the watercress and rocket between four plates. Place the hot, drained fish and potatoes on top, then drizzle with the green sauce.

ROAST NEW POTATO SALAD

This is a good accompaniment to cold roast beef or chicken.

Serves 4 as a side dish

500g new potatoes
3 tablespoons olive oil
6 cloves of garlic, peeled and crushed
the leaves from 6 bushy little sprigs of thyme

For the dressing:
a tablespoon of Dijon mustard
2 tablespoons sherry vinegar
60ml olive oil
a teaspoon of chopped chives

Cut the potatoes into thick slices. Toss them in a bowl with the olive oil, garlic, thyme and some salt and pepper. Scatter them in a baking dish and roast in an oven preheated to 200°C/Gas 6 until golden and tender. This will take a good forty-five minutes, maybe a bit longer, depending on the variety of potato. Shake them about a bit now and again so they do not stick.

Remove from the oven and tip into a salad bowl. Whisk the dressing ingredients together with a grinding of salt and pepper. Toss the hot potatoes gently in the dressing, leave for ten minutes, then serve.

Classic French Potato Salad

This salad is good as it stands, but even better if you add some crisp rashers of bacon, thinly shredded.

To mix a dressing such as this quickly, I sometimes put all the ingredients in a small jar, screw on the lid, and shake till it comes together.

Serves 4 as a side dish

500g waxy potatoes
2 shallots, peeled and finely chopped
3 tablespoons tarragon vinegar
125ml olive oil
chopped flat-leafed parsley

Bring the potatoes to the boil in salted water, turn down the heat and simmer till tender. They must be cooked right through, but firm. Drain them and, when they are just about cool enough to handle, peel off their skins.

Slice them thickly into a salad bowl. Mix together the shallots, vinegar and some salt and pepper and slowly whisk in the olive oil. Stir in the parsley, then toss the warm potatoes in the dressing. Leave for at least half an hour for the potatoes to soak up some of the dressing.

CHICKEN

'It's the skin that does it; all crisp and glistening, and all those gooey, sticky bits underneath ...'

CHICKEN SOUPS AND SNACKS

Tom Yam Gai

Fried Chicken Sandwich

Peter Gordon's Chicken, Buckwheat Noodle,
Garlic and Coriander Laksa

CHICKEN ON THE GRILL

Grilled Mustard and Herb Chicken

Grilled Lemongrass Chicken

SOOTHING CHICKEN

Creamy Roast Chicken Risotto

Coq au Riesling

Chicken and Sweetcorn Chowder with
Smoked Sausage

Chicken with Vermouth, Tarragon and Cream

Chicken Braised with Chicory and Crème Fraîche

A Really Good, Simple Chicken Supper

SIMPLE ROASTS

Chicken with Roast Onion and Thyme Gravy

Roast Chicken with Tarragon Juices

Roast Chicken with Basil and Lemon

Roast Chicken Drumsticks with Honey and Orange

SPICY CHICKEN

Thai Spiced Chicken Wings

Grilled (or Fried) Chicken with Chilli, Lemon and Mint

Green Chicken Curry

REAL CHICKEN

A big, fat, free range chicken is a magnificent thing to unwrap on your return from the shops. Full of promise. We can butter it with generosity, tuck tufts of thyme and bay leaves under its legs and let it roast until its skin is crisp; or we can cut it up and leave it to bubble quietly with mushrooms, cream and wine, or slap it on the bars of a hot grill and brush it with tarragon, mustard and garlic till it shines and sizzles.

The more you pay for your chicken the better it will probably be. It takes a while for a farmer to raise a proper chicken, especially if it has been fed organically. One of the old breeds will have bags of flavour and good strong bones with which to make stock. The flavour will be richer and gamier than that of a cheap, intensively reared bird, and a jolly sight more interesting to eat. You will end up with more for your money.

Whether it is roasted with herbs and olive oil, simmered with spices and cream or baked with newcomers to our shelves like lemongrass and lime leaves, a chicken will rarely let you down. It may be a more expensive supper than pasta but, in my book, it is worth every penny.

TOM YAM GAI

A clear, light, hot and sour soup. The magic of this is that it is both restorative and invigorating yet easy on the stomach. Unless chillies don't like you, that is. Lime leaves are part and parcel of Thai cooking but you may have to make an excursion to your nearest major supermarket or Chinese store to get them (buy a big bunch; they freeze well).

Serves 2

1 chicken breast, skinned
1 litre home-made or ready-made fresh chicken stock
4 spring onions, finely chopped
2 cloves of garlic, peeled and finely chopped
1 stalk of lemongrass, chopped into 2.5cm lengths and slightly
    crushed
3 small red chillies, seeded and thinly sliced
4 lime leaves
1 tablespoon nam pla (Thai fish sauce)
1 teaspoon sugar
1 tablespoon fresh lime juice
1 tablespoon chopped coriander leaves

Bring the chicken breast to the boil in the stock, then turn the heat down to a simmer. Cook until the chicken is tender, about ten minutes, then remove and cut into thin shreds. Set aside, saving the all-important broth.

Add the spring onions, garlic, lemongrass, chillies and lime leaves to the broth and simmer gently for ten minutes. Add the fish sauce, sugar and shredded chicken and continue cooking for three or four minutes. Stir in the lime juice and taste for seasoning, adding a little salt if necessary, then finally stir in the coriander and serve piping hot. Tepid Tom Yam Gai is a friend to no one.

FRIED CHICKEN SANDWICH

When you strip the meat from the bones for this crisp, sticky snack, don't forget the juicy little oysters that lie on the underside where the legs join the carcass.

Makes 1

2 or 3 large handfuls of juicy meat torn from a roast chicken carcass
a small baguette or 2 crusty rolls
1 free range egg, beaten
fine cornmeal or fresh breadcrumbs
50g butter
1 tablespoon olive oil
good quality garlic mayonnaise from a jar
a handful of salad leaves
half a lemon

Tear the meat into bite-sized pieces and split the baguette or rolls in half horizontally. Dip each piece of chicken first into the beaten egg and then into the cornmeal or breadcrumbs.

Melt the butter in a shallow pan, pour in the oil and when it starts to sizzle put in the chicken. Fry over a moderate heat, turning from time to time, until golden. This may only take a minute or two.

Spread the mayonnaise over the cut side of the bread. Be generous. Then add a layer of salad leaves. Fish the pieces of chicken from the hot butter with a draining spoon and slip them on top of the salad leaves. Pour half of the butter out of the pan, squeeze in the juice of half a lemon and let it bubble for a few seconds, then pour it over the chicken. Put on the top half of the bread, press gently and eat immediately, preferably with a bottle of very cold beer.

PETER GORDON'S CHICKEN, BUCKWHEAT NOODLE, GARLIC AND CORIANDER LAKSA

A stunning soup full of vibrant flavours. A meal in a bowl.

Serves 2

2 boned free range chicken thighs
2 tablespoons sesame oil
10–12 garlic cloves, unpeeled
1 medium onion, peeled and finely sliced
2 cloves of garlic, peeled and finely chopped
1 medium carrot, peeled and cut into very fine strips
2 teaspoons peeled and finely chopped fresh ginger
1 mild red chilli, finely sliced
30ml tamarind paste
1 litre brown chicken stock
20ml tamari
150g buckwheat noodles, cooked
a generous handful of coriander leaves

Mix the chicken thighs with the sesame oil and unpeeled garlic cloves, spread them in one layer in an ovenproof dish and cook in an oven preheated to 200°C/Gas 6 for twenty-five minutes. Remove from the oven. Drain the oil and juices into a large saucepan and put the chicken and garlic to one side. Heat the saucepan and add the onion, chopped garlic, carrot, ginger and chilli. Sauté over a moderate heat, stirring from time to time, until the onion has wilted. Add the roasted garlic cloves, tamarind paste and the chicken stock and bring to the boil, then simmer for ten minutes. Cut the chicken thighs into small chunks, add them to the pan and warm them through for a few mintues.

Add the tamari and check for seasoning; add more if needed. Heat the buckwheat noodles in warm water and place in heated bowls. Ladle the laksa broth over the noodles and sprinkle generously with coriander leaves.

GRILLED MUSTARD AND HERB CHICKEN

A storecupboard way with chicken. The chicken sizzles and browns on the griddle, then you pour over the meagre, concentrated dregs of sauce made from rinsing the griddle with the remains of the wine vinegar and mustard marinade. Intensely savoury, it must be eaten very hot, with salt and the squeeze of a lemon.

Serves 2, depending on the size of the chicken pieces

6 large free range chicken thighs
4 tablespoons olive oil
1 tablespoon dried tarragon
a heaped tablespoon of chopped parsley
a heaped tablespoon of smooth Dijon mustard
2 tablespoons red wine vinegar

Turn each chicken thigh skin-side down and slide a small, very sharp knife either side of the bone. With a mixture of the knife and your fingers, loosen the bone from the flesh and then discard it.

Mix the oil, herbs, mustard and vinegar together. Toss the chicken thighs in this and leave them for an hour or more. If you put them in the fridge, you should leave them overnight.

Get a stove-top griddle pan hot. Shake most of the marinade from the chicken and place flat on the griddle. There will be much smoke and sizzling. Cook till the chicken pieces are golden brown outside, turning after about four minutes, and till their juices run clear when pierced with a knife. They will probably take about eight minutes total cooking time, depending on the size of your thighs (or, rather, the size of the chicken's). As you remove the last chicken thigh from the grill, pour any remaining marinade on to the grill pan and just a little water (or wine or stock), let it bubble a bit, then pour it over the chicken. Eat whilst piping hot from the grill, with a little crushed salt sprinkled over them, and perhaps with a little lemon juice.

GRILLED LEMONGRASS CHICKEN

I have a craving for citrus-hot meat dishes. Lime juice, garlic and chillies are what makes this dish such a great fix. I eat this with soft, old-fashioned lettuce leaves, wrapping each piece of chicken up in the lettuce, then popping it in my mouth.

Serves 1 with plain rice

250g free range boned chicken breast
groundnut oil
a squeeze of lime juice
lettuce leaves, to serve

For the marinade:
a stalk of lemongrass, chopped
juice of 2 plump limes
3 cloves of garlic, peeled and crushed
4 small shallots, peeled and chopped
a tablespoon of nam pla (Thai fish sauce)
a teaspoon of sugar
2 small, hot red chillies, chopped
a tablespoon of groundnut oil
a tablespoon of sesame oil
a teaspoon of sesame seeds

Slice the chicken breast into strips about as thick as your little finger and put them in a shallow dish. Mix all the marinade ingredients together and pour the resulting slop over the chicken pieces. Toss them gently, then leave to marinate for half an hour. Longer will not hurt.

Get a stove-top grill pan hot (use an overhead grill if that is what you have). Wipe with a little groundnut oil and add the chicken. Leave to cook for a minute or two on each side, by which time the meat should have turned pale golden in patches and be temptingly fragrant. Eat whilst hot, squeezing over a little lime juice and wrapping each piece in a lettuce leaf.

CREAMY ROAST CHICKEN RISOTTO

As instantly soothing as sucking your thumb, this is the best use I have come across for the chicken carcass facing you in the fridge on a Monday evening. I don't know why I didn't think of it before. The quality of the stock is paramount, so pour water over the chicken carcass and simmer it with a carrot, bay leaf and onion for half an hour or so before you start.

Serves 2 generously

a medium-sized onion, peeled and quite finely chopped
50g (a thick slice) butter
a small palmful of thyme leaves
250g arborio rice
1 litre hot chicken stock
350g leftover roast chicken, torn into lumps
100g crème fraîche
a handful of chopped parsley
Parmesan, grated

Cook the onion slowly in the butter in a heavy, shallow pan over a medium heat. The onion should soften without colouring. It is ready when you can see through it. Stir in the thyme and pour in the rice. Stir the rice through the butter, then add a little of the hot stock. It will come slowly to the boil. Turn the heat down and, stirring occasionally, add ladlefuls of stock as the last one is absorbed. As you add the final one, stir in the roast chicken.

After twenty minutes the rice should be tender but still have a bit of a bite to it. To the tooth, as they say. Stir in the crème fraîche and the parsley (don't leave it out; the flavour of the chopped leaves is wonderful here), then some salt and pepper. Leave it for five minutes, then eat in big platefuls. Grate over a little Parmesan cheese.

Coq au Riesling

This was on the menu at the very first restaurant I worked in. I loved its creamy, winey sauce from the word go and made it every day for months. Once it came off the menu I forgot about it for about twenty years. It suddenly came back to me when I was looking through some old menus. Here it is then, in all its cream- and wine-laden glory. A fabulous dish, especially with a proper green salad (no fancy stuff, thank you) to mop up any sauce left on the plate.

Serves 2

50g butter
a tablespoon of olive oil
100g streaky bacon or pancetta, diced
2 small to medium onions, peeled and chopped
2 cloves of garlic, peeled and chopped
4 joints of free range chicken on the bone
200g small brown mushrooms, halved or quartered
500ml medium-dry white wine such as Riesling
300ml double cream
3 tablespoons chopped parsley

Melt the butter in a heavy-based casserole and pour in the oil. Put in the diced bacon or pancetta and let it colour a little, then add the onions and garlic. Leave to cook over a moderate heat until the onions have softened but not yet coloured. Scoop the bacon and onions out with a draining spoon, leaving behind the cooking juices, then add the chicken pieces. Let them brown lightly on all sides. A moderate heat is best for this but be prepared to add a little more oil if the butter shows signs of browning.

Add the mushrooms and continue cooking for a few minutes, then return the bacon and onions to the pan. Turn up the heat, pour in the wine, bring quickly to the boil and then turn it down to a simmer. Let everything cook at a gentle bubble for twenty-five minutes, turning the chicken from time to time.

Lift the chicken out of the pan and pour in the cream. Season with salt and freshly ground black pepper and stir in the chopped parsley. Continue cooking, at an enthusiastic bubble, until the cream starts to thicken slightly. Return the chicken to the pan. When the chicken is thoroughly hot and the sauce has the thickness of double cream, serve.

CHICKEN AND SWEETCORN CHOWDER WITH SMOKED SAUSAGE

A main course soup, sweet and smoky.

Serves 2 as a main dish

50g, a thick slice of butter
2 small leeks, thinly sliced
a medium potato, peeled and diced
3 large ears of sweetcorn
1 litre home-made or bought ready-made chicken stock
250g free range chicken thighs or breast
150g smoked sausage, skinned
a teaspoon of thyme leaves
100ml whipping cream
2 tablespoons chopped parsley

Melt the butter in a deep, heavy pot and cook the leeks slowly till soft, stirring occasionally. Add the diced potato. Peel the husk from the sweetcorn and cut each corn cob into four chunks. Bring the stock to the boil in a separate pan and add the sweetcorn and the chicken, then turn the heat down and simmer for ten minutes, or until the corn is tender and the chicken lightly cooked.

Cut the sausage into rounds a little thicker than pound coins and drop them in with the softened leeks. Stir in the thyme and continue cooking on a gentle heat. Remove the chicken and sweetcorn from the stock, then pour the stock into the leeks and continue simmering.

Cut the kernels from the cobs (by holding the cob upright and slicing down with a heavy knife) and slice the chicken into thick pieces, then add to the soup with a seasoning of salt and black pepper. Simmer for ten minutes, then stir in the cream and chopped parsley. Bring almost to the boil, stirring often, then serve.

CHICKEN WITH VERMOUTH, TARRAGON AND CREAM

A dish that exploits the magical chemistry between chicken, cream, wine and herbs to the full.

Serves 4

8 free range chicken pieces on the bone, preferably thighs
75g butter
150ml dry vermouth
2 tablespoons tarragon vinegar
300ml double cream
2 heaped tablespoons chopped tarragon leaves
a squeeze of lemon juice

Season the chicken pieces with a little salt and finely ground pepper, then brown them lightly in the melted butter. A large, shallow pan is best for this. The skin should be gold in colour, the butter should be a nutty golden brown, but take care that it does not burn. (If it does, or if there are speckles of brown in it, pour it off and add a little more fresh butter.) Lift out the chicken pieces.

Pour off all but a tablespoon or so of butter. Add the vermouth and tarragon vinegar to the pan, bring to the boil and scrape away at any sticky bits on the bottom of the pan, stirring them into the vermouth. Once the liquid has reduced a little in the pan – a matter of a minute or two – pour in the cream and add the tarragon leaves. Return the chicken and any juices to the pan and simmer gently for fifteen to twenty minutes, stirring from time to time and making certain that the cream does not thicken too much or catch on the bottom of the pan. If the sauce is becoming too thick, add a little more vermouth.

Check that the chicken is cooked through, taste for seasoning, adding salt, pepper and a squeeze of lemon juice, then serve.

CHICKEN BRAISED WITH CHICORY AND CRÈME FRAÎCHE

A straightforward enough recipe – not as complicated as it looks – where the juices you end up with are a heavenly mixture of chicken, bitter chicory and sweet cream. Plain steamed or boiled floury potatoes and green beans are the only accompaniments you will need.

Serves 3

2 tablespoons groundnut oil
a thick slice of butter, about 30g
6 large free range chicken pieces, bone in (drumsticks, thighs, breast)
3 heads of chicory, cut in half lengthways
2 teaspoons brown sugar
3 shallots, peeled and finely chopped
juice of a lemon
125ml medium-dry white wine – something from Alsace would be
    ideal
180ml crème fraîche
a few sprigs of parsley, chopped

Heat the groundnut oil with the butter in a large, deep, heavy casserole, one to which you have a lid. When the butter starts to bubble, carefully put in the chicken pieces – in two batches if you need to – and cook them till they are golden on each side. Try not to move them too often, then you will get a nice browny crust on the skin.

Lift the chicken out of the pan and set aside. If the butter and oil mixture is still in good condition, you can use it for the next bit. If it looks a bit dark, pour it out and add some more, but on no account get rid of the sticky bits on the bottom; that is where much of the flavour is. Put the chicory in the pan, then season with the sugar and some salt and pepper. Let it cook over a moderate heat until the outside leaves start to caramelize and darken and soften – a matter of about five minutes.

Add the shallots and lemon juice, then return the chicken to the pan. Pour over the wine and bring to the boil. Turn the heat down and simmer for about ten minutes, until the wine and cooking juices have reduced a bit. Spoon in the crème fraîche, season with salt and pepper and stir as best you can so that the juices mingle with the cream. Cover with a lid, then put in an oven preheated to 200°C/Gas 6 and leave for about an hour. Move the pieces of chicken and chicory around half-way through cooking.

Lift the chicken and chicory out of the sauce with a draining spoon and put in a serving dish. Return to the oven. Add half the parsley to the sauce with a seasoning of salt and freshly ground pepper and put it over a moderate heat. Let it simmer enthusiastically until it starts to thicken slightly – it should be the consistency of double cream. Add the rest of the parsley, give it a bit of a stir, then pour the sauce over the chicken. Serve with plain, floury boiled potatoes to soak up the juices.

A Really Good, Simple Chicken Supper

Exactly what it says. Serve with mashed potato.

Serves 2–3

6 joints of free range chicken on the bone
butter – about 50g
2 tablespoons olive oil
a large glass of white wine (something not too dry)
4 juicy young garlic cloves, squashed flat in their skins
a good handful of bushy, bright green parsley, chopped
lemon juice
a thick slice (about 30–40g) fresh, cold butter, to finish

Rub the chicken with salt and black pepper. Warm the butter and oil in a heavy-based cast iron casserole dish, one to which you have a lid. When they start to sizzle, put the chicken in, skin-side down. Let the skin colour a little, then turn it over. Over a moderate heat, let it bubble gently in the butter and oil until the skin is sticky and shining and the meat is tender. At the slow pace I suggest, this will take a good forty-five minutes.

Remove the chicken with a draining spoon, tip all but a drop of the fat from the pan (keep it for roasting potatoes) and return the pan to the heat. Turn up the heat, add the wine and let it bubble furiously whilst you scrape up all the crusty, golden goo stuck to the bottom of the pan and stir it into the wine. Return the chicken to the pan and leave to simmer at a mild bubble, covered with a lid.

After eight or ten minutes add the garlic cloves and parsley (this may seem a bit late but we are only after a whiff). Continue cooking for six or seven minutes, adding more wine if it is getting low. It should be thick and sticky, just a little bit more than a goo sticking to the chicken really. Squeeze in a little lemon juice, add a little salt and pepper and fish out the garlic. Transfer the chicken to warm plates, drop the butter into the pan and quickly swirl it round in the few cooking juices left. Spoon the meagre but delectable buttery juice over the chicken.

CHICKEN WITH ROAST ONION AND THYME GRAVY

Mashed potato – the proper stuff made with hot milk and plenty of butter – is what is needed here (see page 40).

Serves 4

1.5–2kg free range chicken
75g butter
4 medium onions, peeled
4 plump cloves of garlic, peeled and sliced
the leaves of 6 bushy sprigs of thyme
3 bay leaves
250ml chicken stock

Preheat the oven to 230°C/Gas 8. Rub the chicken inside and out with half the butter and season with black pepper and a little salt. Cut the onions in half and then cut each half into about six segments. Warm the remaining butter in a roasting tin in the oven for a minute or two, then add the onions and toss with the garlic, thyme leaves and bay. Place the chicken on top of the onions and return to the oven for fifteen minutes. Turn down the heat to 190°C/Gas 5 and continue roasting for forty-five minutes or until the juices run clear when the flesh of the bird is pierced with the point of a knife.

Lift the bird from the roasting tin and leave in a warm place to rest. Pour off some of the fat from the tin, then put the tin over a moderate heat and add the chicken stock. Bring to the boil, check for seasoning and leave to simmer gently for ten minutes whilst you carve the chicken. Spoon the roast onion gravy over the chicken and serve.

ROAST CHICKEN WITH TARRAGON JUICES

Sometimes I am happy to spend all day making a wonderful sauce for a chicken supper. Other times I just want something as simple as this – a plump, free range bird roasted in butter, its pan juices seasoned with just salt, pepper and a sprinkling of chopped fresh herbs. Serve an old-fashioned green salad, lightly dressed with oil and lemon juice, on the side.

Serves 4–6

a free range chicken, about 1.8 kg
90g butter
a good fistful of tarragon leaves (about 30g), chopped
3 cloves of garlic, peeled
a glass of white wine

Place the chicken in a roasting tin. Mash the butter and most of the tarragon together and season with black pepper and salt. Crush the garlic cloves to a mush and stir into the herb butter.

Smear the chicken all over, inside and out, with the herb butter, then pour the wine into the roasting tin. Place in an oven preheated to 220°C/Gas 7 for fifteen minutes, then turn the heat down to 190°C/Gas 5 and roast for a further forty minutes. Baste the bird from time to time with the juices from the pan, adding a little more wine or water if need be.

Turn the oven off and leave the chicken for ten minutes before carving. Serve with the roasting juices, which you have thrown the rest of the tarragon into and checked for seasoning.

ROAST CHICKEN WITH BASIL AND LEMON

A fragrant roast for which you will need fruity olive oil (it need not be extra virgin, just good-quality plain olive oil) and a fine bird. Use lots of basil – the tougher-leafed variety is better than most of the flaccid affairs sold on the plant – and a medium-dry white wine, one that you will drink with the roast.

Serves 2

6 free range chicken pieces, bone in (thighs, breasts, drumsticks)
olive oil
2 juicy cloves of garlic
a lemon
a large handful of basil (about 30 leaves)
a wine glass of white wine

Season the chicken and put the pieces in a roasting tin. Pour over enough olive oil to moisten them and make a shallow pool in the tin. Squash the garlic in its skin and tuck it in with the chicken. Squeeze the lemon over the chicken and drop the empty lemon shells in too. Roast for thirty minutes in an oven preheated to 200°C/Gas 6, then tear up the basil leaves and toss them about a bit with the chicken. Return to the oven for ten minutes. Remove from the oven, pour the wine over the chicken, then put the roasting tin over a hot flame and let the wine bubble for a minute. Eat with a few green salad leaves – such as Little Gem lettuce – to mop up the sticky, aromatic pan juices from the plate.

A Chicken in the Oven

There are few more reassuring sounds than the low crackle and spit of a chicken roasting in the oven. A sound that says all's well. Brought to the table in its well-worn roasting dish, a golden chicken surrounded by roast potatoes stuck to the pan with the chicken's golden goo, the bird is a feast in every sense of the word. Nothing sounds, smells or tastes quite as friendly as a roast chicken.

Nigella Lawson massages her chicken – a majestic, organically reared free-ranger – with olive oil or butter and sticks half a lemon up its bottom before salting it and putting it to roast at 200°C/Gas 6 for twenty minutes per 500g, with an extra half hour for good measure. She retains the lemon 'out of habit' and, as she says, 'to make the kitchen smell like my mother's, with its aromatic, oily-sharp fug'.

Nigella is generous with the seasoning, sometimes adding more olive oil, shallots and garlic – two whole heads of garlic and twenty unpeeled shallots for four – half-way through cooking. They steam in their skins, 'which on the shallots are like twists of brown paper. Eat them by pressing on them with a fork, letting the soft, mild, creamy interior squeeze out on to your plate.'

It is no affectation to season the chicken from within. Some people lay a bunch of tarragon inside, still secured with its string; others rub the corrugated rib cage with salt and butter and tuck in a bay leaf too. If, like me, you are the sort who tugs at the slippery, gooey bits of the bird that others leave behind, then you will be glad you seasoned every little nook and cranny.

The more I cook, the less cream I use. But chicken and cream were made for one another, especially if you add a glass or two of white wine and some mushrooms or chopped aniseed herbs such as tarragon or fennel. Sometimes, when I feel in need of something utterly cosseting, money no object, I will stir wine and chopped tarragon into the pan- juices of a roast bird, bring it to the boil and stir in a glug or two from the cream pot. Still at a boil, I scrape at the gooey pan-stickings with a flat-edged wooden spoon and stir them into the bubbling cream. Roast chicken with tarragon cream gravy, anyone?

The next day, the cold bones and the jelly that holds them to the plate will make a soup to warm and soothe. Just boil them all up with bright green parsley stalks and a young carrot for sweetness. An onion will deepen the flavour and lend a jewel-bright colour. Turn down the heat and simmer gently before straining and seasoning. Pure, golden broth. Perhaps I might scatter over a few stellini pasta, the little stars twinkling in the hot amber soup.

Tear the flesh from the bones and you have the start of a sauce for Monday's pasta. Just add mushrooms and cream. Or what about starting from scratch – frying chicken joints till their skin glistens, then adding softened onion, garlic and pancetta to start a white version of coq au vin? Finish with baby mushrooms, cream and a whole hand's worth of chopped bushy parsley. Or toss the cold chicken pickings in egg and crumbs and fry them till crisp, then stuff them into a baguette with garlic mayonnaise and soft lettuce.

Soothed enough? Then let's get out the aromatics. Chicken loves all the hot-sour-tart tastes of the East. I find even the lowliest chicken responds to an hour or two in a marinade of oil, stalks of lemongrass shredded into rings, hair-fine strips of lime leaf, a chopped chilli or two (you can leave the seeds in, Thai-style) and the wrung-out juice of a grated thumb of ginger. Slap it on a smoking cast-iron grill pan so that the skin blackens here and there against the bars, whilst the rest slowly cooks to a glossy gold.

Roast Chicken Drumsticks with Honey and Orange

Food for friends. It works well made in larger quantities too, for a party, say. The point is to cook the chicken, turning from time to time, until it is really, really sticky.

Serves 4

12 large free range chicken drumsticks
olive or groundnut oil
2 heaped tablespoons honey
2 medium-sized oranges

Put the chicken drumsticks in a roasting tin and drizzle over a little oil – just enough to moisten them and form a thin film on the bottom of the tin. Add the honey. Cut one of the oranges in half and slice the other thickly. Squeeze the halved orange over the drumsticks, then tuck the slices and the empty orange shells under the drumsticks. Season with salt and black pepper, then roast in an oven preheated to 200°C/Gas 6 for fifty minutes to an hour (turning once or twice during cooking), until thoroughly sticky. Eat with your fingers.

THAI SPICED CHICKEN WINGS

Serves 2–4

a tablespoon of nam pla (Thai fish sauce)
juice of a lemon
a teaspoon of sugar
2 plump garlic cloves, peeled and crushed
a tablespoon of groundnut or olive oil
12 free range chicken wings

For the dipping sauce:
6 tablespoons rice vinegar
4 tablespoons sugar
a tablespoon of dark soy sauce
2 small red chillies, seeded and very finely chopped
a tablespoon of coriander leaves, very finely chopped
juice of a lime

Make a thin paste of the fish sauce, lemon juice, sugar, garlic and oil. Season it with ground pepper, then pour it over the chicken wings. Set them aside for an hour or more.

Make the dipping sauce: bring the vinegar and sugar to the boil in a small pan and leave it to boil until it becomes syrupy, about five minutes, maybe less. Remove from the heat, stir in the soy sauce, chillies, coriander leaves and lime juice, then leave to cool. It will become thick and sticky.

Grill the chicken wings until golden and starting to crisp. You can do this either under an overhead grill or on the barbecue (making sure they are cooked right through) or, if you prefer, you can roast them for about thirty-five minutes in an oven preheated to 200°C/Gas 6.

Serve them hot or cold, with the dipping sauce.

Grilled (or Fried) Chicken with Chilli, Lemon and Mint

You can grill the chicken, as I do here, or fry it. The choice is yours. On the grill the smell reminds me of the open-air food stalls of Marrakech that reek of mint, lemon and smoke. Fried, the chicken tends to stay a little moister but you lose out on the deep smokiness that makes grilled food so tempting. Decisions, decisions. Either way, it is an exciting way to cook little bits of bird. Some couscous, well buttered and flecked with coriander and sultanas, makes a lovely, soothing accompaniment to the spicy chicken.

Enough for 2

400g free range chicken off the bone (breast, thigh meat, whatever)
1 medium-sized hot red chilli (or 2 bird's eye chillies), seeded and
    chopped
1 heaped teaspoon crushed dried chillies
2 cloves of garlic, peeled and chopped
2 pinches of saffron stamens
a handful of mint leaves (20 or so)
4 tablespoons olive oil
juice of 1 large or 2 small lemons
hunks of lemon, to serve

Cut the chicken into thin strips roughly the size of a finger and put them in a china or glass basin.

Whizz the fresh and dried chillies, the garlic, saffron, most of the mint, olive oil and most of the lemon juice in a blender or food processor till you have a thick, speckled, bright red, orange and green slush. Pour it over the chicken and toss gently. Set aside for half an hour for the chicken to take up some of the flavours of the marinade.

Heat a ridged grill pan and lightly oil it. When it is hot, add the strips of chicken, and any marinade clinging to them, and fry for three or four minutes on each side, till they are golden brown in patches. They will be firm to the touch and sticky. Watch that the chilli does not burn; if it shows any sign of singeing, then turn down the heat. Season with a little salt and the remaining lemon juice and mint. Serve with hunks of lemon.

GREEN CHICKEN CURRY

Green curries are one of my favourite suppers. They are vibrant yet soothing (that's chillies and coconut milk for you). I have fiddled around with green curry recipes for several years now, adding and subtracting ingredients at whim, and have finally settled on this one, which is particularly hot and creamy. It seems like a lot of work, yet is surprisingly quick to make. The ingredients involve a trip to a major supermarket. Those who have access to a Thai or Chinese grocer's can pick up everything in ten minutes.

Don't be tempted by the commercial curry pastes available in the shops. Even the best can't shake a stick at one you make at home. A fresh one is so much more vital and aromatic. You will find it keeps for a few days in the fridge if tightly sealed.

Green Chicken Curry

Continued

Serves 4 with rice

750g free range boned chicken breasts or thighs

3 tablespoons groundnut oil

200g chestnut mushrooms, quartered

400ml tin of coconut milk

400ml home-made or chilled ready-made chicken stock

8 lime leaves

1 tablespoon nam pla (Thai fish sauce)

1 tablespoon bottled green peppercorns, drained

the leaves from a large bunch (about 20g) basil, shredded

15g coriander (leaves and stalks), roughly chopped

For the curry paste:

the tender heart leaves of 4 lemongrass stalks

6 medium-hot green chillies, seeded and chopped

3 cloves of garlic, peeled and crushed

5cm piece of galangal or ginger, peeled and chopped

2 shallots, peeled and finely chopped

4 tablespoons chopped coriander

a teaspoon of ground cumin

a teaspoon of ground coriander

a teaspoon of chopped lime zest

a tablespoon of lime juice

a tablespoon of nam pla (Thai fish sauce)

$\frac{1}{2}$ teaspoon ground black peppercorns

For the curry paste, slice the lemongrass finely. Put it in a food processor with all the remaining curry paste ingredients and whizz to a thick paste, pushing the mixture down from time to time with a rubber spatula. Transfer to a glass or china dish, cover tightly (otherwise it will taint everything in the fridge) and refrigerate.

For the curry, cut the chicken into finger-thick strips. Warm the oil in a casserole and, when hot and sizzling, add the chicken strips and let them colour slightly on all sides. You will need to do this in batches to avoid crowding the pan. Lift them out with a draining spoon and throw in the quartered mushrooms. Fry till golden brown, adding more oil if needed. Pour in the coconut milk and stock, then add the lime leaves, 4 heaped tablespoons of the curry paste, the fish sauce, peppercorns and half of the chopped herbs. Bring to the boil, then turn the heat down and and simmer for ten minutes, stirring from time to time.

Return the chicken to the pan with a further tablespoon of the paste and simmer for five to six minutes. Stir in the last of the herbs and serve.

SAUSAGES

'I want a sausage that is sticky outside and juicy within. I want its skin to be tight, glossy and deep golden brown, and to be coated in that savoury, Marmite-like goo that only comes with slow cooking.'

SAUSAGE SUPPERS

Fatty Pork and Lentils

Toad with
Browned Onion and Madeira Gravy

Pasta with Spicy Sausage,
Basil and Mustard

Sausage and Potato Pie

Sausages and Onion Sauce

Nigella Lawson's Chorizo with Potatoes

Alastair Little's Salsicce e Peperoni

Paul Heathcote's Black Pudding and
Lancashire Cheese Hash Browns

A VEGETARIAN SAUSAGE

White Bean sausages with
Anchovy Mayonnaise

IN SEARCH OF THE PERFECT SAUSAGE …

I want a sausage that is sticky outside and juicy within. I want its skin to be tight and deep brown, and to be coated in that savoury, Marmite-like goo that comes with slow cooking.

It must be a proper butcher's sausage. A butcher stands or falls by his sausages. And it must be a plump one – no skinny chipolatas for me, thank you. Some fancy a smooth, bland banger but I insist on one that is coarsely ground with plenty of herbs (nothing fancy – a bit of thyme and parsley will do) and a generous hand with the pepper. It must be juicy. There is no joy in a dry sausage.

A sausage for breakfast would be a treat indeed, fighting as it does against the morning rush and the modern attitude to healthy eating. It is a wonderful way to wake up. Especially when someone else has risen early and the smell is already wafting up the stairs.

A Sausage in the Pan

The difference between good eating and quite ordinary eating is often only the matter of a tiny detail. A good sausage – a perfect sausage – must be very, very hot. So hot that you have to jostle it round your mouth with your tongue. It should also have the sort of skin that 'pops' in the mouth, exuding savoury, peppery, herby juices.

So, a good-eating sausage is very hot, with tight skin and lots of seasonings. It must also be sticky. The scrumptious goo that is built up on the outside is the whole point of eating a sausage. It comes only with slow cooking and cannot be properly achieved by grilling.

Matthew Fort is a man with a passion for sausages. They have been his Saturday morning breakfast for most of his life. He insists: 'The proper cooking of sausages is a tranquil, almost meditative business. It involves no violence or agitation of any kind. Above all, this means you must never, ever, under any circumstances whatsoever, prick a British sausage of any kind of quality. It does not require or deserve such treatment. If you do prick, you will only allow a good deal of the natural juices to flow out during cooking, making the inside drier and lessening the flavour.

'Just lay those gleaming, pristine links across the centre of the frying pan and leave them there, gently cooking, for a very long time (long enough to make a pot of tea, take it upstairs to your slumbering partner, rouse him or her, share a few agreeable moments of repose, wash, dress, and slope downstairs again) – anything between forty minutes to an hour. It is only through frying, and slow frying at that, that you allow the meat to heat through slowly and thoroughly, encouraging the polite transformation of flavours, the retention of essential juices, and the fat to leach out through the semi-permeable skin.

'At the end of the process the outside should have tanned to a deep, glistening bronze, the contents of which will have consolidated to a moist, sweet-flavoured mouthful yielding gently to the teeth.'

Mr Fort's recipe for the perfect sausage is the best way to guarantee a banger beyond reproach. But it is essential to start out with the right banger. Like cheese and bread, supermarkets have never really got this subject right. Here and there are examples of a good supermarket sausage but they are very few and far between. I have a theory that sausage recipes, like cakes and pastry, lose something when made in large quantities.

But there are some very good sausages around. My local butcher, Chris Godfrey in Highbury, North London, makes his on the premises and, like many proper butchers, takes pride in producing a sausage that people queue for. You can see the freckles of herbs and pepper under the skin, they are generously sized sausages, yet there is nothing fancy about them. Just carefully made, old-fashioned butcher's sausages.

The other good hunting ground for bangers is Italian delicatessens. They often have them hanging up (unless the local health inspectors are on the prowl) all linked with string. These tend to be on the spicy side. Just the thing for toad in the hole (which I have, since childhood, abbreviated to toad). Italianate bangers often contain garlic, chilli and fennel. This is no bad thing for a supper sausage, but unthinkable for a Sunday morning sausage.

The smell of a chubby, sticky link sizzling softly in its pan makes me yearn for mash. Mountains of buttery, creamy mashed potato. If I am having a 'fatfest' then I shall make a proper job of it. But what is sausage and mash without onion gravy? Thick, glossy, brown onion gravy. Oh, and mustard, I simply must have mustard with my sausage.

BEYOND BREAKFAST

I think sausage and mash can be one of the most perfect suppers on earth. It goes without saying that both the sausage and the mash must be right. By which I mean the sausage must be an old-fashioned pork sausage and the mash must be the light and fluffy kind made with butter and hot milk and floury potatoes (see page 40), otherwise I think the meal will be too heavy. There are many occasions on which the richer type of mash made with a somewhat waxy potato (and often favoured by chefs in very good restaurants) is suitable. But I don't think this is one of them.

Call me old-fashioned but I really don't buy into the newfangled sausage fad. Anything from sun-dried tomatoes and olives to venison with cranberries turns up in a banger nowadays. I would much rather have a well-made pork butcher's sausage. Find a truly good one and I am not sure you will need the fancy stuff.

The garlicky Toulouse sausages can be wonderful, though, with a velvety onion sauce and mashed potatoes, as can the strings of spicy ones hanging up in Italian grocer's shops. Serve them slowly fried with a handful of noodles that you have tossed in warm cream and shredded basil.

We can cook with a banger, too. Sausage hotpot is a pretty good thing to come home to on a winter's night. The classic recipe with tomatoes and potatoes is fine enough but I sometimes prefer an earthier, more fatty version for keeping out the cold. It is then that I get out the lentils and belly pork too. Steaming food for a freezing night. There are few things as warming as a hot sausage.

FATTY PORK AND LENTILS

A great, big, porky casserole for a freezing winter's night. Few recipes will warm you like this one – the unctuousness of the pork fat will probably mean you might like a frisée and watercress salad afterwards.

Serves 2–3

50g Italian lardo or pancetta, diced
500g boned pork belly, cut into large cubes
6 spicy butcher's sausages
2 medium onions, peeled and roughly chopped
4 cloves of garlic, peeled and chopped
a few herbs, such as thyme, bay etc.
150g brown or green lentils, rinsed
300ml stock or water
a squeeze of lemon, if necessary
a handful of chopped parsley leaves

Cook the cubes of lardo or pancetta in a large casserole over a moderate to high heat until they give off enough melted fat in which to fry the pork. When the fat is hot, add the cubed pork, leaving it to colour lightly and stirring occasionally. Remove each batch as it turns golden.

Add the sausages and brown them lightly, then remove. Cook the onions and the garlic, together with a couple of bay leaves, and some sprigs of thyme if you have them, in the fat until they are soft and golden, a matter of ten or fifteen minutes on a moderate heat.

Put the pork and sausages back in the pan with the onions and herbs, season with a little salt and pepper, then cover tightly with a lid and put in an oven preheated to 180°C/Gas 4 for half an hour.

Add the lentils to the pot with the stock or water. Return to the oven, covered, and continue to cook for forty minutes or so, until tender. Remove, stir and taste for seasoning; it will need salt, pepper and possibly a squeeze of lemon. For once, a heavy scattering of parsley would not go amiss.

TOAD

I am not sure that getting fancy with a classic dish like toad in the hole can come to any good. I have added a seasoning of mustard because I think it flatters the sausage, and wrapped the bangers in ham to make the dish more substantial, but that is as far as I go. This dish has a homely quality to it that defies meddling. There are those who like a bit of batter with their sausages and those who prefer a bit of sausage with their batter. I am one who is fondest of the batter – both the crusty bits on top and the soggy underneath – so I make my toad in a wide dish to give plenty of room around the sausages for the batter to swell. And then, of course, there's onion gravy.

Serves 4

2 free range eggs
125g plain flour
150ml milk mixed with 150ml cold water
1 level tablespoon grain mustard
6 fat, herby pork sausages
100g thinly sliced prosciutto, pancetta, serrano ham or even thin
    streaky bacon
3 tablespoons dripping or lard

Mix the eggs, flour, milk, mustard and some salt and pepper together with a whisk, beating out any little lumps of flour as you go. The consistency should be about that of ordinary double cream, but no thinner. Leave to rest for fifteen minutes.

Cut the skin from each sausage and peel off. Wrap each piece of skinned sausage meat in a piece of prosciutto or whatever you are using. Put the dripping or lard in a baking tin – I use a 28 x 21cm roasting tin – and place in an oven preheated to 220°C/Gas 7 until it is smoking. Pour in the batter – it will sizzle softly in the hot fat – then arrange the sausages in the batter. Get it into the oven and bake for twenty-five to thirty minutes, till puffed and golden. Serve with Browned Onion and Madeira Gravy (see page 117).

BROWNED ONION AND MADEIRA GRAVY

I first intended this gravy to be poured over my toad in the hole but now make it for mashed potatoes, potato cakes, liver and braised vegetables (it is sensational with celery that has been braised in vegetable stock). It keeps for a couple of days in the fridge and is glorious poured, steaming hot, over bubble and squeak.

a very thick slice (about 75g) butter
2 large onions, peeled and thinly sliced
flour, no more than a level tablespoon
75ml Madeira, Marsala or red wine
250ml stock
Worcestershire sauce

Melt the butter in a heavy-based pan, add the onions and cook over a low heat till golden and soft. Now continue cooking, covered with a lid, until the onions are truly brown and soft enough to crush between your fingers.

Stir in a level heaped tablespoon of flour and cook for a few minutes until it has lightly browned, then pour in the liquids. Season with salt and pepper and Worcestershire sauce and bring to the boil. Turn the heat down so that the gravy bubbles gently and leave for about fifteen minutes, stirring from time to time.

PASTA WITH SPICY SAUSAGE, BASIL AND MUSTARD

This recipe appears in my book *Real Cooking*. I include it again here because it is featured in the television series that this book accompanies. I do think, though, that it is worth repeating. For this version I used orecchiette, which takes longer to cook – it will need about twenty minutes.

For 2

4 spicy Italian pork sausages
olive oil
4 handfuls (about 250g) of dried pasta (any tube or shell shape or
    even pappardelle)
a glass of white wine
dried chilli flakes, a pinch or two
a small handful of chopped basil, plus a few leaves to garnish
a tablespoon of Dijon mustard
200ml double cream

Put a large pan of water on to boil for the pasta. Split the sausages open and take out the filling. Warm a little olive oil in a frying pan, just enough to lubricate the bottom. Discard the sausage skin, crumble the meat into the hot pan and fry till sizzling and cooked through, about five minutes. Salt the water generously and add the pasta.

Pour the wine into the sausage pan and let it bubble a little, scraping at the sausage goo stuck to the bottom of the pan. Stir in the chilli flakes and chopped basil. Add a little salt and the mustard, pour in the cream and bring slowly to a simmer. Cook for a minute or two, stirring now and again.

When the pasta is tender, about nine minutes after coming to the boil, drain and tip into the creamy sausage sauce. Serve piping hot, garnished with a few basil leaves.

Sausage and Potato Pie

Don't even think of making this lovely, crumbly pie with anything but really tasty, well-seasoned sausage meat. It may be better to buy your favourite butcher's sausages and undress them. The pastry is particularly short. I see no point in making anything that isn't.

Serves 4

175g plain flour
40g lard
40g butter
about 2 tablespoons cold water
350g new potatoes, scrubbed and thinly sliced
a medium onion, peeled and thinly sliced
a little oil or pork fat
500g sausage meat or herby butcher's sausages, skinned
a little beaten egg and milk

Make the pastry: put the flour in a food processer, add the fats in little cubes and a good pinch of salt. Whizz to fine crumbs, then tip out into a bowl. Sprinkle over a very little water – start with no more than a tablespoon – and bring the dough together with your hands to form a soft ball. Refrigerate for half an hour.

Drop the potatoes into boiling salted water and cook for five minutes. Drain them thoroughly and set aside. Cook the sliced onion in the oil or pork fat till soft and nutty gold. Roughly crumble the sausage meat into the cooked onion. Mix in the potatoes and pack loosely into a 23cm rimmed pie plate.

Roll out the pastry gently, then wet the rim of the pie plate with water or some of the beaten egg and milk. Lift the pastry up with the aid of the rolling pin and place it on top of the sausage meat. Press the edges down hard to the rim. Brush with some of the egg wash and cut two little steam holes in the top. Bake in an oven preheated to 200°C/Gas 6 for thirty-five to forty minutes, till golden brown.

SAUSAGES AND ONION SAUCE

Sticky sausages and creamy, savoury sauce. Serve in the classic manner with mounds of very smooth mashed potatoes (the sloppy sort that includes hot milk creamed in with the butter).

Serves 4

3 medium Spanish onions, peeled and finely sliced
75g butter
8–12 plump, herby sausages
a little dripping, lard or groundnut oil
275ml double cream

Cook the onions slowly in the butter in a shallow pan set over a low heat. It will take thirty minutes, maybe even longer, for them to colour, though they should not brown. This is a sweet sauce and dark onion will send it bitter. Stir the onions regularly but not so often that you stop a thick, sticky goo developing under them.

Start to fry the sausages slowly in a heavy frying pan with a little of the fat. They will take a good twenty-five minutes. Tend to each pan from time to time, turning the sausages so that they colour nicely on all sides, becoming sticky and caramelized.

When the onion is soft enough to squash between your fingers, stir in the cream, mixing in the goo at the bottom of the pan. It will darken and enrich the sauce. Grind in a little salt and pepper. You will not need much. When the cream has bubbled a little and the sauce is deepest ivory beige, serve it with the hot sausages.

Nigella Lawson's Chorizo with Potatoes

This stew is both plain and yet intensely flavoured: the thickly sliced, fat-pearled, paprika-bright sausages ooze oily and orange into the sherry-spiked broth. You need proper, semi-dried (sometimes called fresh) sausages rather than the drier, stouter-waisted salame. What you must guard against are those tight-fleshed, too lean and unyielding, so-called 'Spanish-style' chorizo.

Serves 4

1 tablespoon oil
1 small to medium onion, peeled and finely chopped
400g semi-dried chorizo sausages
3 cloves of garlic, peeled and finely chopped
1 bay leaf
100ml dry sherry
1kg small waxy potatoes
chopped fresh coriander

Put the oil in a wide rather than deep pan that can go in the oven – an oblong enamelled casserole or suchlike – and put on the hob over a medium to low heat. Add the onion and cook for five minutes or so, until beginning to soften. While it is cooking, slice the chorizo into fat coins. Add the garlic to the pan and cook, stirring, for another couple of minutes. Add the chorizo, bay leaf and sherry and stir. Slice the potatoes in half and add to the pot. I just stand by the pot, knife in hand, slicing them in one at a time. When they are all in, stir and then pour over water from a just-boiled kettle to cover, but only just; don't worry about the odd potato poking above water level. Simmer for ten minutes and taste for seasoning.

Put the dish, uncovered, in an oven preheated to 200°C/Gas 6 and cook for thirty to forty minutes. Remove, ladle into bowls, and sprinkle over some chopped fresh coriander as you hand them round. You need lots of (unbuttered) bread with this, but not much else – perhaps a pale, crunchy and astringent salad after.

ALASTAIR LITTLE'S SALSICCE E PEPERONI

Serves 4

2 medium red and 2 medium yellow peppers
400g spicy Italian sausages, for example, luganega
2 medium onions, peeled and cut into rings
4 tablespoons extra virgin olive oil
half a dozen basil leaves

Remove the skins from the peppers by putting them on a hot griddle over the highest heat possible. Turn occasionally until the skins are completely black and blistered. Take them off the griddle and put them into a colander in the sink. Under cold running water, peel off the skins and let the colander catch all the black skins rather than blocking the sink. Try to avoid immersing the peppers or you will lose the grilled flavour.

Dry the peppers and place them on a chopping board. Cut each pepper in half and remove and discard the stems, seeds and pith. Cut the peppers into strips.

Put the sausages into an ovenproof dish or pan and moisten with a little water. Put into an oven preheated to 180°C/Gas 4 for twenty-five minutes, checking and turning them as they cook. In a frying pan, heat the olive oil over a medium heat. Add the onion rings and cook until they have started to crisp and blacken. Add the pepper strips and mix together.

Tip the vegetables on to the sausages, toss together and season with the basil leaves. Return to the oven for ten minutes before serving.

PAUL HEATHCOTE'S BLACK PUDDING AND LANCASHIRE CHEESE HASH BROWNS

As much as I like black pudding I rarely seem to do much with it beyond throwing it in the frying pan. This recipe of Paul Heathcote's is a revelation, and will convert even those who think they don't like this gorgeously rich, dark sausage. Much depends on the quality of the pudding itself, so go for the best you can find.

Makes 4

500g Maris Piper potatoes
a teaspoon of chopped chives
a teaspoon of roughly chopped parsley
1 free range egg white
4 slices of good black pudding
125g Lancashire cheese, cut into 4 slices
oil for deep- or shallow-frying

Boil the potatoes in their skins till only just soft, then drain and peel. Grate them into a bowl and mix in the chopped herbs. Add a pinch of salt to the egg white, beat lightly with a whisk or fork to loosen it, and mix with the grated potato. Season with salt and pepper.

Divide the mixture into four. Pat out each quarter of the mixture into a circle slightly larger than the black pudding. Place a slice of pudding in the middle and a slice of cheese on top. Fold and shape the potatoes over the stuffing neatly, so that it is thoroughly enclosed.

Deep-fry at 160°C until golden brown or shallow-fry for two to four minutes on each side. Serve with a poached egg and some Hollandaise sauce.

White Bean Sausages with Anchovy Mayonnaise

A sausage, but one without meat.

Serves 4

250g cannellini beans
1 large shallot or small onion, peeled and finely chopped
2 cloves of garlic, peeled and finely chopped
2 small red chillies, seeded and chopped
1 small free range egg
75g mature farmhouse cheese such as Lancashire, grated
a little flour
beaten egg and fine, dry breadcrumbs for coating
groundnut oil for frying
lemon wedges, to serve

For the mayonnaise:
4 large salted anchovy fillets or 8 smaller ones, rinsed
a large cupful/200ml mayonnaise (home-made or from a bottle)
2 cloves of sweet, juicy young garlic, peeled and chopped
juice of half a lemon
$\frac{1}{2}$ teaspoon cayenne pepper

Soak the cannellini beans overnight in deep, cold water. They will swell up to twice their size by morning. Pour off any remaining water, cover with fresh water and put on the heat to cook at a lively simmer for about forty-five minutes. By this time they will be soft but not squashy. They are done when you can crush them between your fingers. Drain them thoroughly.

For the mayonnaise, mash the anchovy fillets to a paste and stir into the mayonnaise with the other ingredients. It will keep in a screw-top jar for a few days. Indeed, probably longer.

Mash the beans with a potato masher or whizz them, for a few seconds only, in a food processor. Stir in the shallot or onion, garlic, chillies, egg and grated cheese, then season with generosity with both salt and black pepper. You can put in a bit of chilli pepper if you wish. Leave to cool. The mixture should be a stiffish paste.

Roll the mixture into thick, short sausages. Put some flour on your hands as you roll them, otherwise you will get in a right old mess. You should end up with about twelve. Drop them into the beaten egg, then the crumbs and then fry in hot, deep oil until crisp, about six minutes. Eat hot with huge dollops of the anchovy and garlic mayonnaise and a wedge of lemon.

GARLIC

'Running out of garlic would be as unthinkable as running out of salt, pepper or olive oil …'

GARLIC BASICS
Roasting Garlic
Roast Garlic Pureé
Seasoned Olives
Parmesan Garlic Bread

GARLIC WITH VEGETABLES
Oyster Mushrooms with Roasted Garlic
Roast Pepper Salad
Baked Chicory with Parmesan
Grilled Aubergine Salad
Nigella Lawson's Pea and Garlic Soup
Mushroom and Spinach Korma
Flageolet Salad

GARLIC WITH FISH AND MEAT
Garlic Scallops
Peter Gordon's Grilled Scallops with
Sweet Chilli and Crème Fraîche
Prawns with Garlic
Greek Fish Soup with Orange and Courgette
Crisp Fish with Garlic, Chilli and Basil
Pork with Mushrooms and Garlic (and Potato Cakes)
Pork with Cashews, Lime and Mint
Grilled Marinated Lamb
Alastair Little's Chicken with
Forty Cloves of Garlic
A Rough, Garlicky, Country Terrine

SUMMER GARLIC

Round about late May or early June the first garlic appears in the market. The very first from Italy or France is plump and white, its skin a soft green, brushed with anything from the faintest pink to the deepest mauve. I pounce on it. Tied in threes, the bulbs are fat and pale and the smell is at first barely detectable.

At home, I peel back the waxy skin and pull out the slippery white cloves. Each one has its own thick skin, still wet and pliable. Tucked inside are the sweetest, juiciest nuggets of garlic. So firm and crisp I want to eat them like slices of new season's apple. This is the garlic I want for cutting in half and rubbing on thick, crisp toast, or for slicing thinly and tucking between the silky folds of a roasted pepper, or for rubbing round the salad bowl. This is the garlic for scenting summer mayonnaise, for stuffing into a chicken as it roasts, for using with generosity. This is the sweet, mild garlic of romance . . .

WINTER GARLIC

The season for green summer garlic is all too short. By September, August even, the bulbs are losing their sweetness and starting to dry. Their skin crisps, their flesh darkens. This is the dry garlic that will have to see us through to spring. More intense and less juicy, it needs tempering with heat and slow cooking. This is the garlic for casseroles, curries and baking. This is the stuff I slice as thinly as possible and stew with onions and olive oil as the bones of a casserole. Chopped into little nibs or sliced as thin as a fingernail, it will be fine in a stir-fry. Pounded with salt, it still has enough juice for scenting a garlic butter for mushrooms or bread.

As the winter wears on I cook fewer and fewer dishes where garlic is the point of them. Its pungency can be unpleasant, its sweetness gone. At this time I also watch my garlic carefully. Approaching Christmas it often starts to sprout, as if it was still in the ground. These tiny green shoots need teasing out with the point of a knife. They are invariably bitter and I find them indigestible. You can still use the plumper cloves in a stew. Once they have become dry and beige and their smell rank, they are fit only for the bin.

ROASTING GARLIC

Roast garlic emerges from the oven as sticky, golden nuggets – sweet, mellow and as soft as butter. A whole head of summer garlic, split through the centre, drizzled with everyday olive oil and scattered with thyme leaves, takes on an especially mild sweetness. Sweet enough to spread on toast. Dry winter garlic, still plump and without any green shoots, will roast successfully too, though I blanch mine in boiling water first for a milder flavour. After nearly an hour in a hot oven it should be soft enough to squash between your fingers. It is pure pleasure to squeeze a button of caramelized garlic from its skin. It slips out with one little squeeze.

This is when the cloves can be stirred into the pan juices of roast lamb or pork or dropped into the rich sauce of a casserole half-way through cooking. Mash them to an ivory ointment with flakes of sea salt in a pestle and mortar and you have a thick, honey-hued butter to do with as you will.

Roast Garlic Pureé

4 large, juicy heads of garlic (the huge heads of elephant garlic
  would be ideal)
a wine glass of olive oil
thyme and bay leaves

Slice the heads of garlic across their diameter. Put them in a shallow
baking dish and turn them cut side up. Tip over the olive oil and tuck
in a few sprigs of thyme and a couple of bay leaves. Bake in an oven
preheated to 180°C/Gas 4 for forty minutes, basting from time to time,
till they are golden and the cut edges are very slightly caramelized. The
cloves must be soft enough to squash between your fingers.

Scoop the soft cloves from their skins with a teaspoon and remove
the tiny brown root. Mash to a purée using a pestle and mortar
(easiest), a wooden spoon or, if you have cooked a large number of
heads, a food processor. You should get a good heaped tablespoon
from each head.

Now we have a jar of fragrant, honey-coloured garlic cream to play with:

• Spread the neat purée thinly on toasted baguette as an appetizer.
• Mix with a little cream cheese as a spread for toast.
• Make a suave, rich sauce by mixing 2 tablespoons of garlic purée
with a tablespoon of olive oil, a tablespoon of Marsala and 100ml
double cream in a small pan over a low heat. Cook till thick, then
season with salt. A good sauce for grilled poultry.
• Add a spoonful to a casserole during cooking. It is already cooked
and can be added whenever you like.
• Use as a storecupboard alternative to chopped garlic in stir-fries.
• Store in an airtight jar in the fridge, with its surface covered by a thin
layer of olive oil. It will keep for a week or two.

Seasoned Olives

Olives with a waft.

4 cloves of juicy garlic, squashed in their skins
a tablespoon of red wine vinegar
a teaspoon of finely chopped thyme leaves
2 tablespoons extra virgin olive oil
half a teaspoon of crushed dried chillies
250g black olives

Put the garlic, vinegar, thyme, olive oil and chillies in a clean, dry Kilner jar. Add the olives and shake the jar, then seal. Leave for at least forty-eight hours, though a week will be even better.

Parmesan Garlic Bread

Eating rarely comes any better than crunching into a slice of hot, crusty, garlic bread. Except when you add freshly grated Parmesan to the garlic butter. The idea here is to get the bread well and truly sodden with garlicky butter whilst the crust crisps up. The cheese should form thin strings as you tear one piece of bread from the next. This is the sort of food you want (and which is just about possible to produce) when you are having a very, very good time (you know what I mean).

Enough for 4

100g butter, softened
3 juicy garlic cloves, peeled and finely chopped or crushed
a fistful of chopped parsley, green and lush
50g coarsely grated Parmesan
a small baguette

Mash the butter to a cream in a small bowl – you can do it with a pestle and mortar but a china bowl and wooden spoon will work just as well. Mix in the garlic, parsley and grated Parmesan.

Put the baguette on a large piece of silver foil (or whatever its proper name is) and cut deep slashes into it. Try not to cut right through the loaf.

Push lumps of the garlic butter into the cracks. Be generous – your challenge is to get 100g of butter (that's nearly half a pack) to go into one extremely small loaf. Wrap the loaf loosely in the foil and bake in an oven preheated to 220°C/Gas 7 for twenty minutes. Unwrap the foil and bake for a further five minutes, till the bread has gone a little crunchy on top yet is soaked with cheesy, garlicky butter.

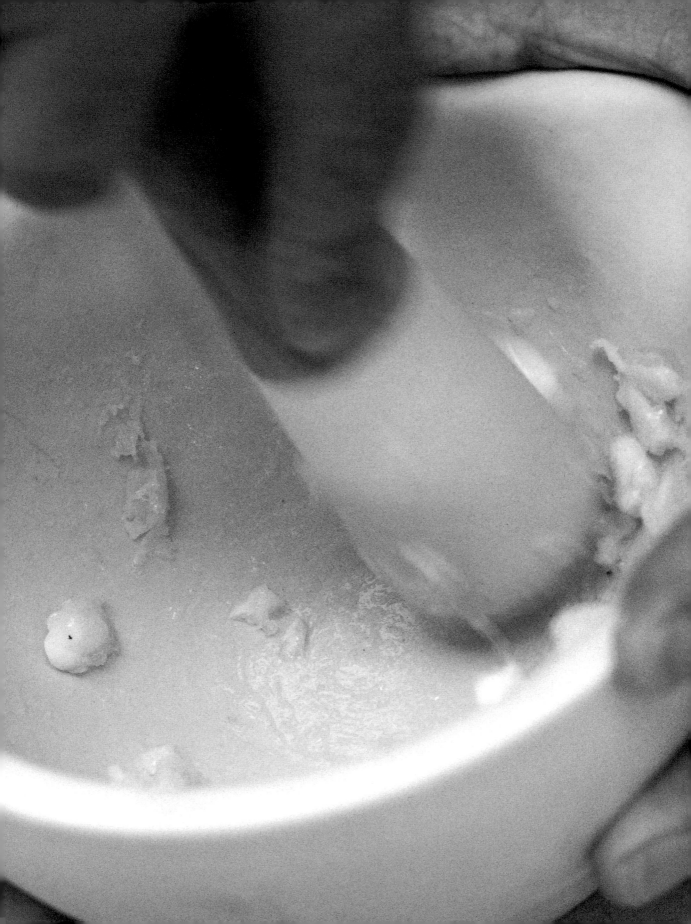

Oyster Mushrooms with Roasted Garlic

Serves 2 as a light meal

a plump head of garlic
200g oyster mushrooms
75g butter
a few sprigs of thyme

Peel the garlic cloves and bring them to the boil in a small pan of water. Drain them and bring to the boil again in fresh water. Let them simmer for five minutes, then drain.

Put the mushrooms into a baking dish and smear with the butter. Season them with salt and pepper. Tuck the boiled garlic cloves all around the mushrooms and scatter with the thyme leaves.

Roast in an oven preheated to 200°C/Gas 6 for twenty minutes. It is important that you baste the mushrooms from time to time to stop them drying out. The butter will take on the scent of thyme and garlic and should be spooned over the mushrooms as they cook. The garlic cloves will colour slightly and, after twenty minutes' roasting, will be soft enough to squash with light pressure.

Serve the mushrooms from the dish with their buttery cooking juices and some of the sweet roasted garlic. A few salad leaves and some bread for the pan juices will be all you need.

AND IT'S GOOD FOR US...

I eat for pleasure rather than my health. I would rather eat a small portion of something I really like – say, pork crackling or crisp, golden chicken skin, than a plateful of lean roast pork or skinless chicken. My main gripe against those who take it upon themselves to police our diet is that they fail to understand the pure pleasure of good eating, be it the smell and flavour of their cooking or the feel of it in their mouths. What is the point of eating a piece of Parma ham without its sweet, aromatic fat or roast duck without its crisp and juicy skin? It is as if they don't actually like food, as if they feel guilty about eating something that is sexy to devour. So imagine my joy when I found out that garlic, about which I am something of a zealot, is positively good for me.

Not only does garlic smell heavenly as it fries, bakes or roasts; not only does it add aroma and warmth to our cooking; not only does it turn the simplest piece of meat or vegetable into something quite sublime but it is actually doing me good. The 'food police' inform me that garlic can help lower blood cholesterol, contains sulphides that are thought to help prevent cancers, and can prevent my blood clotting. What more could I ask?

The use of garlic has rocketed in recent years. Even thirty years ago we were only likely to meet it in restaurants or on holiday. Now it is as much a part of our cooking as salt and pepper. I cannot be the only one who finds its smell truly tantalizing when it hits the smoking oil of a hot wok. When it is baking slowly in the oven, perhaps in a gratin with potatoes and cream or roasting with oil and thyme, and the sweet aroma gently permeates the room, I find it comforting in the extreme. Garlic can excite or soothe as the mood takes us.

ROAST PEPPER SALAD

When you roast peppers you get the most gorgeous, sweet, almost caramelized roasting juices. Just imagine eating them mixed with the warm sweetness of soft roast garlic. Some crusty bread and a soft goat's cheese will turn this into a light summer lunch.

Serves 4 as a salad

6 large, ripe red peppers
a head of young garlic
extra virgin olive oil

Put the peppers into a shallow roasting tin with the garlic, broken up into cloves but not peeled. Rub the peppers with a little olive oil, then roast in an oven preheated to 180°C/Gas 4, until the skins are heavily tinged with black, a matter of thirty to forty minutes.

Remove the peppers, halve them and, whilst they are still warm, peel away the skin and discard it. Scrape away any seeds but be careful to retain any juices from both the peppers and the roasting tin. Place the peppers in a shallow dish.

Squeeze the garlic from its skin – it should slide out – and mash it with a little sea salt and a grinding or two of black pepper. Stir in the juices from the red peppers, then enough olive oil to bring the dressing to the consistency of double cream. Drizzle the dressing over the peppers and leave to cool to room temperature.

Serve with bread to mop up the juices.

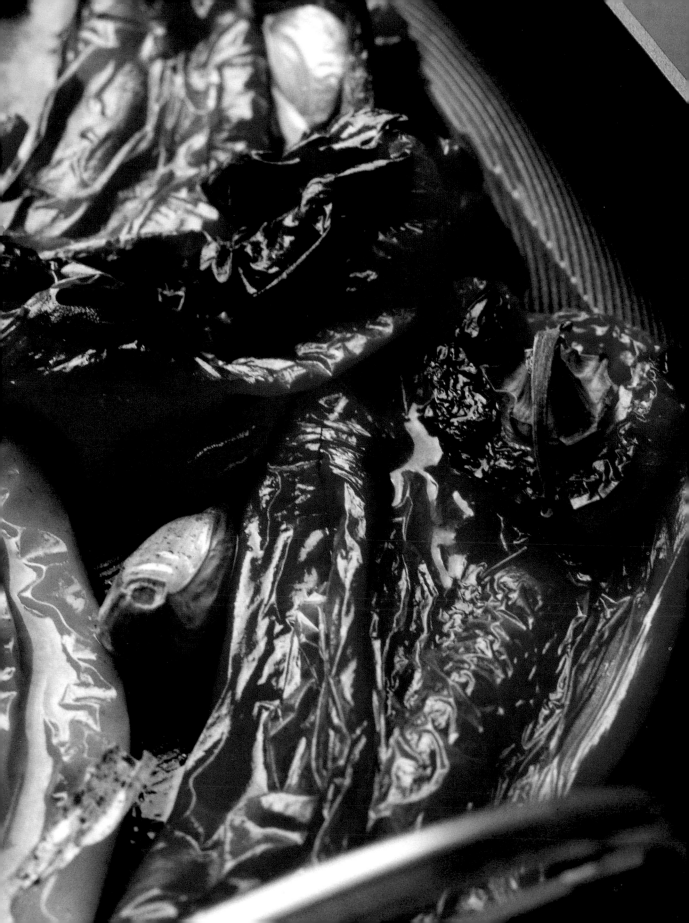

Baked Chicory with Parmesan

A lovely recipe this, the chicory going sticky and golden in the butter with the faintest hint of garlic.

Serves 4 as a side dish

4 large heads of chicory
75g butter
2 cloves of garlic, squashed flat but not peeled
a small lemon
6 tablespoons fine, white, fresh breadcrumbs
5 tablespoons finely grated Parmesan

Trim the heads of chicory, cutting off any imperfect leaves and trimming the root. Slice each head in half from root to tip. Warm the butter in a casserole over a moderate flame, then place the halved chicory in it cut side up so that it sits snugly inside. Tuck in the garlic. Let both chicory and garlic colour slightly in the hot butter, then turn them over. Cover with a lid and leave to cook slowly in the butter. Take care that the chicory does not colour too quickly. Once the underside turns pale gold, squeeze over the lemon, then scatter the crumbs and grated Parmesan evenly on top.

Transfer, still covered, to an oven preheated to 190°C/Gas 5 and bake for about thirty minutes, until the cheese has melted. Serve hot, as a side dish.

GRILLED AUBERGINE SALAD

When aubergines are sliced and grilled they take on a deep, smoky flavour and, with olive oil and garlic, make a salad redolent of the Mediterranean.

Serves 4

2 large aubergines
extra virgin olive oil
2 large garlic cloves, peeled and finely sliced

For the dressing:
juice of a lemon
4 tablespoons extra virgin olive oil
the fine leaves of 3 or 4 bushy sprigs of dill, chopped

Slice the aubergines lengthways into thick tongues. You will get about six slices from each one. Put them in a shallow dish with the garlic and pour over enough olive oil to soak them through, then leave for about half an hour.

Get a ridged cast iron grill pan hot over a moderate flame. Put the aubergine slices, a few at a time, on the grill and, without moving them, leave to cook slowly until their flesh is soft, with clear dark lines left by the grill pan. Turn them once. Cooked liked this they will develop a mild smoky flavour, though it will be more intense if you cook them outside over charcoal. As each one gets tender, lift it off with a wide, flat metal slice and place on a serving plate. Make sure they are all thoroughly tender.

While the next batch is cooking, make the dressing by mixing the lemon juice, olive oil and chopped dill with a little salt and black pepper. Pour the dressing over the aubergines while they are still warm. Set aside for fifteen minutes (although they will come to no harm if you leave them longer). Serve them warm or at room temperature, but not chilled.

Nigella Lawson's Pea and Garlic Soup

A beautiful green soup. Both fresh and subtle, it is as good with or without the cream, and also makes a very fine chilled soup.

Serves 2

a head of garlic
2 teaspoons olive oil
200g frozen peas
25g butter
2 tablespoons freshly grated Parmesan
200ml vegetable or chicken stock, heated
150ml double cream, or to taste

Lop the top off the head of garlic; you want to see the tops of the cloves just revealed in cross section. Cut out a square of foil, large enough to make a baggy parcel around the garlic. Sit the garlic in the middle of it and drizzle with the olive oil. Make a loose parcel around the garlic, sealing the edges of the foil. Put in an oven preheated to 200°C/Gas 6 for about an hour, until soft.

Cook the peas in boiling salted water as usual. Drain and tip into a food processor, squeeze in the soft cooked cloves of garlic, add the butter and Parmesan and half of the stock. Process to a creamy purée. Pour the mixture into a saucepan and add the remaining stock. Check the flavour and add cream to taste. Heat gently, season to taste with salt and pepper and serve.

MUSHROOM AND SPINACH KORMA

This recipe is a good example of how garlic is used as a backnote to other aromatics and spices. This is a voluptuous vegetable supper, and less trouble than it might at first appear.

Serves 2–3

50g butter

2 medium onions, peeled and sliced

3 large cloves of garlic, peeled and thinly sliced

a knob of ginger, about the size of your thumb, peeled and grated

a teaspoon of ground cumin

15 cardamom pods, seeds removed and crushed

$\frac{1}{2}$ teaspoon ground turmeric

$\frac{1}{2}$ teaspoon chilli powder

2 cinnamon sticks

2 bay leaves

650g assorted mushrooms

50g shelled hazelnuts, toasted

350g leaf spinach, tough stems removed

50g golden sultanas

150g thick natural yoghurt

150g crème fraîche

2 tablespoons chopped coriander leaves

Melt the butter in a deep pan, add the onions, garlic and ginger and cook for about five minutes, until golden. It is essential not to burn the butter, so add a little oil if it appears to be darkening. Add the spices and bay leaves and continue frying, stirring regularly, for two or three minutes to cook the spices. Meanwhile, cut the larger mushrooms into big pieces, though you can leave oyster mushrooms whole. Add the mushrooms to the pot. Cook the mixture for a few minutes till the mushrooms soften, then stir in 225ml water and the hazelnuts. Bring to the boil, then turn down the heat and simmer for fifteen minutes, covered with a lid.

Meanwhile, wash the spinach and put, still thoroughly wet, into a saucepan – it will cook in its own steam. Cook for two minutes, shaking occasionally, till wilted. Drain and squeeze out the water. Stir the spinach and sultanas into the curry, simmer for a couple of minutes, then mix the yoghurt and crème fraîche together and stir them into the mushrooms, bringing almost to the boil. Season to taste with salt and pepper. When the korma is thoroughly hot, but not quite boiling (it may curdle if it boils), stir in the chopped coriander and serve.

Flageolet Salad

A big-flavoured salad with a loud, bright dressing that begs to be eaten out of doors on a hot summer's day.

Serves 6

300g dried flageolet or cannellini beans
a head of garlic, cut in half horizontally
a large lemon, cut in half
a stick of celery, cut into three
2 or 3 bay leaves

For the dressing:
3 anchovy fillets, rinsed and finely chopped
2 plump cloves of young garlic, peeled and finely chopped
5 tablespoons extra virgin olive oil
1 tablespoon lemon juice
a handful of basil leaves, torn to pieces
a tablespoon of finely chopped young mint leaves
about 20 flat parsley leaves, chopped

Soak the beans overnight in cold water, then drain. Put them in a deep pan, tucking amongst them the garlic, lemon halves, celery and bay. Pour plenty of water over the beans and bring to the boil. Do not salt them till after cooking. They will take anything from thirty minutes to an hour, depending on their age. New-season beans always take less time to cook. When they are nearing tenderness, add salt to the cooking water. When the beans are quite soft to the touch (ignore the silly fashion for crunchy beans – they will just give you indigestion), drain them and then dress them while they are still warm.

In a bowl or mortar, mash the anchovies and garlic with a little ground pepper. Slowly pound in the oil, lemon juice and herbs to give a thick green slush. Toss the beans in the dressing and leave for at least thirty minutes at room temperature before serving.

Garlic Scallops

The difference between even the simplest thing being good and being sublime is often a matter of the most minute detail. Here it is essential to get on with things, cooking the scallops quickly over a high heat. The crux comes when you serve them – the butter must be hot and frothing and heavily fragrant. You should waste not one second before you tuck in.

Serves 2

3 tablespoons olive oil
8 juicy scallops, with their roes
50g butter
4 cloves of garlic, peeled and finely chopped
a small handful of parsley leaves, roughly chopped
lemon halves, to serve

Warm the olive oil in a shallow pan till it starts to sizzle. Season the scallops with sea salt and black pepper, then drop them into the oil. They may splutter. Do not move them for at least a minute. During this time they will form a sticky, golden crust on their underside. Peep to check it is there, then turn them over and cook the other side. They should be done in two or three minutes.

Whip them out quickly and put on to hot plates. Add the butter to the pan – it should melt immediately – then when it starts to foam add the garlic. Swirl the garlic round the pan, throw in the parsley and, whilst all is frothing, pour over the scallops. Take them to the table straight away. Serve with lemon halves.

GREEK FISH SOUP WITH ORANGE AND COURGETTE

A big-flavoured, garlicky fish soup. It is worth taking a few minutes to check over the fish, making sure that the fishmonger has scrupulously scraped away all the scales. I use large-boned fish for this – grey mullet, red mullet and a hunk of monkfish. The fish should be cleaned but left on the bone, then you can slice it into large chunks (little pieces will collapse into the soup). It takes about an hour to make from start to finish, and offers a bowl of clear, sweet soup and a plate of lightly cooked fish to follow.

Serves 4 as a main dish

2 medium onions, peeled and coarsely chopped
3 cloves of garlic, peeled and sliced
1 medium leek, cleaned and cut into thin rings
olive oil
1kg mixed fish, cleaned and gutted but left on the bone
2 medium carrots, diced
2 stalks of celery, diced
a medium courgette, diced
1 teaspoon crushed dried chilli
1 level teaspoon saffron threads
500g tomatoes, seeded and chopped
a couple of bay leaves
a strip of orange zest
juice of an orange
a handful of flat parsley leaves, chopped
toasted slices of French bread and garlic mayonnaise
    (see page 36), to serve

Cook the onions, garlic and leek slowly over a moderate heat in a little olive oil, stirring from time to time. After ten or fifteen minutes they will have softened but they should not colour.

Cut the fish into thick pieces, chopping right through the bone. Rinse thoroughly.

Stir the carrots, celery and courgette into the onions and leek and continue cooking until they start to soften. Add the chilli and saffron, stir and leave for a minute, then add the tomatoes and bay leaves. Simmer for ten minutes over a low heat, stirring occasionally. This slow cooking will give plenty of juice.

Stir in the orange zest, orange juice and 500ml of water and bring to the boil, then turn down to a simmer and cook for twenty minutes, covered with a lid, before introducing the fish. Once the fish is tender enough to just fall from the bone – mine took about twelve minutes add the parsley (this is not purely for garnish). Serve the orange-coloured broth first, with toasted French bread and garlic mayonnaise to float, followed by a plate of the chunks of fish and vegetables, moistened by a spoonful of the broth. Use the soup bowls for the fish bones.

CRISP FISH WITH GARLIC, CHILLI AND BASIL

Crisp fish, hot, garlicky sauce.

Serves 2

groundnut or vegetable oil for deep-frying
2 tablespoons cornflour
4 pieces of hake or haddock fillet (not too thick),
  total weight about 500g
a little groundnut oil
4 plump cloves of garlic, peeled and finely sliced
3 small, hot red chillies, seeded if you wish and finely chopped
4 spring onions, shredded
a tablespoon of light soy sauce
a tablespoon of nam pla (Thai fish sauce)
a good pinch of sugar
a handful of basil leaves
a handful of coriander leaves, roughly chopped

Put enough oil into a deep-fat fryer to cook the fish fillets and heat it to 190°C. Put the cornflour on a plate and dredge the fish fillets through it, patting them to make some of the cornflour stick. Fry the fish till golden, turning it in the oil as it cooks. It should be done in three or four minutes. Lift out and drain on kitchen paper.

Pour a little groundnut oil into a hot wok, just enough to make a small puddle in the bottom. Get it very hot, then add the garlic, chillies and spring onions. They should sizzle and pop. Stir quickly as they cook. Watch carefully that the garlic does not burn – it should go a nutty brown within a minute or two. Add the soy, nam pla, sugar and a couple of spoonfuls of water (or use stock if you have it), then stir in the basil and coriander leaves.

Put the fish on warm plates and pour over the hot sauce. Eat straight away.

Pork with Mushrooms and Garlic

Serves 2

4 teaspoons light soy sauce, plus a little more later
4 teaspoons white wine vinegar
4 teaspoons sugar
250ml home-made or chilled ready-made chicken stock
2 teaspoons cornflour, plus some for dredging
250g pork loin
150ml groundnut oil
350g small brown mushrooms, cut into quarters
3 small, hot red chillies, seeded and finely sliced
a knob of ginger as big as your thumb, peeled and cut into thin shreds
4 juicy cloves of garlic, peeled and chopped
3 shallots, peeled and chopped
4–6 tablespoons roughly chopped coriander

Mix the soy sauce with the vinegar, sugar and stock. Stir the cornflour into 2 tablespoons of water till dissolved, then stir into the stock.

Cut the pork loin into thin slices, then toss them in cornflour and a generous pinch of salt.

Heat the oil in a wok. When it is hot, add the pork. Stir and fry till the edges have caramelized. Keep the heat high. Scoop out the pork with a slotted spoon and set aside, then add the mushrooms. Fry till golden brown, a matter of a minute or two, then remove and add to the pork.

There should be a little oil still left in the wok; if not, then add a little more and get it hot. Add the chillies, ginger, garlic and shallots. The smell of the garlic should fill the kitchen immediately. It is almost the whole point of the dish. Stir and fry, fry and stir, till the garlic is deep gold and soft. Add the pork, mushrooms and stock. Keep stirring as the mixture thickens, add a few shakes of soy, then throw in the coriander and serve with rice or the crisp potato cakes opposite.

POTATO CAKES

450g floury potatoes, peeled
2 heaped tablespoons plain flour
1 small egg, beaten
50ml groundnut oil
a thick slice of butter

Grate the potatoes finely – a food processor will do it in seconds. Squeeze out most of the water with your hands, then break up the grated potato in a basin and mix with the flour, beaten egg and a little salt.

Heat the oil and butter in a shallow pan over a moderate to high heat. Squash the potato into four round patties about as big as the palm of your hand. Fry till golden and crisp, then turn and cook the other side. Lift out and drain on kitchen paper. You can keep them warm while you make the pork if you don't feel like battling with two pans at the same time, but they will lose a little of their crispness.

Place potato cakes on each plate, then pile the pork and cooking juices on top of each one. Serve immediately.

PORK WITH CASHEWS, LIME AND MINT

A hot and refreshing stir-fry. Serve with fried rice.

Serves 2

400g pork fillet
6 tablespoons groundnut oil
90g unsalted cashew nuts or peanuts
4 spring onions, finely chopped
4 cloves of garlic, peeled and finely chopped
a 4cm knob of ginger, peeled and finely shredded
4 small, hot red chillies, seeded and finely chopped
zest and juice of 3 big, juicy limes
2 tablespoons nam pla (Thai fish sauce)
a handful of mint leaves, chopped
a handful of basil leaves, torn to shreds

Slice the pork fillet into pieces about as thick as your little finger, then cut them into short strips. Get a wok really hot over a high flame and pour 3 tablespoons of the oil into it. Once the oil is really hot – you will probably hear it crackle – add the pork and cook for three or four minutes, till it is golden brown in patches. Stir it from time to time during cooking, otherwise it will not brown properly. If it produces too much juice (which it shouldn't if your pan is hot enough), tip most of it away and carry on cooking. The heat should be high throughout.

Meanwhile, chop the nuts quite finely. When the meat is browned and sizzling, tip it on to a warm plate with any cooking juices, return the wok to the heat and, when it is really hot and smoking, add the remaining oil. As soon as it is hot add the spring onions, garlic, ginger and chillies and fry, stirring almost constantly for a minute or two.

Tip in the nuts, stir-fry for a minute or two, then return the meat and any juices to the pan. Stir in the lime zest and juice and the nam pla and fry for two minutes, then stir in the herbs. Serve immediately.

BREAD

'Only the generous can make

a sandwich worth eating.'

HOT SAVOURY SANDWICHES

Toasted Smoked Mackerel Sandwich

Spiced Indian Chicken Baguette

Prosciutto and Fontina Pastries

Steak Sandwich

Chicken Satay Sandwich

OTHER SUBSTANTIAL SANDWICHES

Nigella Lawson's Hot Mushroom Sandwich

Peter Gordon's Muffaletta

Hot Mozzarella Focaccia

SWEET SANDWICHES

Toasted Chocolate Panettone Sandwich

Chocolate and Vanilla Ice-cream Croissants

Summer Berry Mascarpone Sandwich

SANDWICHES

There are few days when bread does not pass my lips. There is something about biting into the soft, doughy crumb of a loaf that is instantly satisfying, even before it is swallowed. Whatever the weather, there must be a loaf in the house. It makes me feel secure.

There might be a floury, crisp-crusted *pain de campagne* or a chewy, close-textured sourdough. There might be a bag of white sliced, a soft, floury slipper of ciabatta or an organic wholemeal. There might even be a loaf of home-made dough, all wobbly and unprofessional. Whatever, there will be bread. There must be bread.

More often than not, that bread will be eaten in the form of a sandwich. No snack has yet been devised that is so eagerly devoured by the hungry, especially when it is a bacon sandwich late at night. I rarely get fancy with a sandwich, and my repertoire is simply a small collection of tried and trusted favourites – old friends – rather than some manic bid to build hundreds of wacky butties.

Above all, I like my sandwiches hot, where the bread has been toasted or the filling is straight from the pan or the oven. It could be chips, smoked fish and cream, hot frankfurters or melted chocolate.

Then again, it might be a slice of steak with its golden fat and garlicky butter, or perhaps a layer of melted cheese and prosciutto. Then again, it might not be encased in slices of bread but in puff pastry or pitta.

Some sandwiches are best left to the professionals. Amongst these I would include the salt beef sandwiches of London's East End, New York's pastrami on rye and the club sandwiches that always seem to taste best when ordered from room service in a large international hotel. But many are even better at home, particularly the ones filled with melting cheese or ice-cream, or those that involve dipping the bread into hot fat, like Nigella Lawson's sensational hot mushroom bap, or a classic bacon sandwich – probably the best sandwich in the world.

Toasted Smoked Mackerel Sandwich

Makes 2

4 slices of hot brown toast
butter
Worcestershire sauce
2 smoked mackerel fillets, skinned and roughly mashed
a teacupful of grated Cheddar cheese
2 tablespoons double cream

Spread the toast rather generously with butter and shake over a few drops of Worcestershire sauce. Stir the smoked mackerel fillets together with the cheese and cream. Add more cream if necessary to make a creamy paste. Spoon the mixture on to two pieces of the buttered toast, flash under a heated grill till it starts to bubble, then top with the other two slices and cut each sandwich into four. Eat immediately.

Spiced Indian Chicken Baguette

Makes 2 large sandwiches

8 large free range chicken wings
groundnut or olive oil for frying
2 small, hot red chillies, seeded and finely chopped
3 thin spring onions, chopped
2 cloves of garlic, peeled and crushed to a paste
a knifepoint of ground turmeric
2 small, crusty baguettes or large baps
a little sugar
juice of a lemon
mayonnaise, about 4 heaped tablespoons

Salt and pepper the chicken wings. Heat enough oil to cover the bottom of a shallow pan, add the seasoned chicken and as soon as one side of the wings has coloured a little, turn them over and cook the other side for a minute or two. Turn down the heat, partly cover with a lid and leave over a moderate heat for about thirty minutes or until the wings are cooked right through. You may have to add more oil from time to time. Lift the chicken wings out on to kitchen paper to drain. When cool enough to handle, slip the meat from the bones – it should fall away easily – then set aside.

Mash the chopped chillies, spring onions, crushed garlic and turmeric to a paste with a few drops of the oil. Split the bread in half and toast the cut sides under the grill. The effect is better if you tear them carefully rather than cut them with a knife. Cook the spice paste in the pan for a minute or two, using a little more oil if need be. Take great care not to let it burn. Put the boned chicken back in the pan for a second and stir till coated with the spice paste. Season with a little more salt, a pinch of sugar and the lemon juice. Slather the toasted bread with mayonnaise, pile the hot chicken on to half the bread and sandwich with the remaining pieces. Eat straight away.

PROSCIUTTO AND FONTINA PASTRIES

Wafer thin and deeply savoury, these squares of puff pastry filled with cheese and ham must be eaten hot – straight from the baking tray. Just the sort of thing for a Saturday lunch by the cooker. If you use the ready-rolled sheets of pastry available in the supermarket you will have to roll it even thinner, as it is invariably too thick for these. The crust should be wafer thin.

Makes 4

375g ready-rolled puff pastry
smooth Dijon mustard
120g fontina or Gruyère
90g prosciutto crudo, sliced on the thick side
a little olive oil
grated Parmesan

Cut the pastry in half and roll one piece thinly into a rectangle approximately 40 x 30cm (it must be really thin). Cut the pastry in two long rectangles. Spread each one with a little mustard – about two heaped teaspoons each. Slice half the cheese thinly and cover one half of each pastry rectangle with it, leaving a gap round the edge. On top of that place pieces of the ham, leaving enough for the second piece of pastry.

Brush the edges of the pastry with olive oil, then fold the bare halves over the cheese and ham, pressing the edges down to seal. You should have two thin, squarish parcels. Transfer these to a baking sheet and repeat with the second half of pastry. Refrigerate for half an hour.

Remove the pastries from the fridge, brush them with oil and dust with grated Parmesan. Bake in an oven preheated to 225°C/Gas 7 for ten to twelve minutes, till slightly risen. Check that the underside is crisp; if not, carefully turn the pastries over and cook for a few minutes longer. Eat straight away, while the cheese inside is still hot.

STEAK SANDWICH

The only time I ever eat beef is when it is cooked in such a way as to combine a deeply savoury crust with a very pink and juicy centre. In other words, steak rather than stew (I loathe brown beef). This is a special-occasion snack or solitary supper.

Enough for 2

two 200g pieces of rump steak, cut only about 1cm thick
olive oil
a small baguette or piece of ciabatta, split

For the butter:
50g butter, at room temperature
a little lemon juice
2 tablespoons chopped parsley
a small clove of garlic, peeled and crushed to a paste with
  a little sea salt
a teaspoon of smooth Dijon mustard

Mash the butter, lemon juice, parsley, garlic and mustard together. Place the steaks on a plate and rub them on both sides with olive oil and a little black pepper. Put a ridged griddle pan on a moderate heat to warm. Warm the bread either in the oven or on the griddle before you cook the steaks.

Grill the steaks for a couple of minutes on each side, seasoning them with salt as they cook. Spread the bread with a little of the butter and put any of it that remains on top of the cooked steaks. Whilst they are hot, sandwich them between the warm bread. Eat immediately, pressing so that the butter and mustardy juices mingle and soak a little way through the warm bread.

CHICKEN SATAY SANDWICH

Occasionally, I don't want a sandwich in a hurry at all. I want to take my time. In which case this is usually the one I make. There is something about the sweet, salty sauce and the soft, doughy bap that appeals.

Enough for 4 baps

450g chicken thigh or breast meat
2 garlic cloves, peeled and finely chopped
2 tablespoons sesame oil
2 tablespoons golden caster sugar or granulated sugar
2 tablespoons rice wine
4 soft, floury baps

For the peanut sauce:
a shallot, peeled and chopped
2 cloves of garlic, peeled and crushed
a small thumb of ginger, peeled and grated
a stem of lemongrass, tender part only, shredded
a tablespoon of vegetable oil
3 small, hot chillies, seeded if you wish, finely chopped
a teaspoon of curry powder
150g coarse-textured, natural peanut butter
3 tablespoons chopped coriander
a little sugar

Cut the chicken into strips barely thicker than your little finger. Toss it with the garlic, sesame oil, sugar and rice wine. Leave for about an hour. Cook the strips of chicken on a hot griddle till golden and sweet.

For the sauce, soften and very lightly brown the chopped shallot, garlic, ginger and lemongrass in the oil over a moderate heat. Stir in the chillies and curry powder and continue cooking for a couple of minutes. Add the peanut butter and 250ml water and bring to the boil. Season with the coriander and sugar to taste (you will probably need only a teaspoon or so). Pile the chicken, tossed generously in the peanut sauce, on to a soft bap, perhaps with a little lettuce if that suits you.

NIGELLA LAWSON'S HOT MUSHROOM SANDWICH

I shall be eternally grateful to Nigella Lawson for introducing me to her recipe for hot mushroom sandwich. It is, as she suggests, 'a memorable solitary supper and is satisfyingly beefy, mustardy, garlicky and buttery.' If you ask me, I reckon it is one of the best – and simplest – ideas of all time.

For 1

'Get a large, flat field mushroom, put it in a preheated 200°C/Gas 6 oven covered with butter, chopped garlic and parsley for about twenty minutes. When ready, and the garlicky, buttery juices are oozing with black, cut open a soft roll, small ciabatta or bap, or chunk of baguette even, and wipe the cut side all over the pan to soak up the pungent juices. Smear with Dijon mustard, top with the mushroom, squeeze with lemon juice, sprinkle with salt and add some chopped lettuce or parsley as you like; think of this as a fungoid – but strangely hardly less meaty – version of steak sandwich. Bite in, with the juices dripping down your arm as you eat.'

Peter Gordon's Muffaletta

Peter Gordon first came across this sandwich ten years ago at the Central Grocery in New Orleans, where it was apparently created in 1906. The beetroot is his own addition. The original recipe calls for sourdough bread, though I have used an unorthodox focaccia loaf before and it worked well enough.

Enough for 6

a round sourdough loaf, about the size of a dinner plate
150ml extra virgin olive oil
200g pitted green olives, finely chopped
6 sun-dried tomatoes in oil, drained and sliced
4 large vine-ripened tomatoes, sliced 5mm thick, sprinkled with a
    little salt and black pepper
a handful of sliced spring onions
a handful of chopped parsley
100g capers in brine, drained
4 medium artichoke hearts in oil, drained and sliced 5mm thick
400g Emmenthal or Gruyère, sliced
200g raw beetroot, peeled and finely grated
100g pancetta, finely sliced and baked or grilled till crisp

Cut the loaf horizontally in half. Drizzle the bottom half with some of the olive oil. Layer all the ingredients on top, in the order above, then drizzle over the rest of the oil and season with a little salt and freshly ground pepper. Top with the remaining half of the loaf.

Wrap in waxed paper or baking parchment and weigh down with something heavy, such as a pile of plates, for fifteen minutes till compact. Unwrap and cut into wedges.

HOT MOZZARELLA FOCACCIA

This is a cross between a pizza and a sandwich. It is essential that the focaccia is not too thick and cakey as some of them are. Though if that is what you have it will still be fine enough, but it might be better to bake it rather than grill it.

Serves 4 as part of a light lunch

350g buffalo mozzarella
100ml extra virgin olive oil
a handful of basil leaves
2 bottled red chillies, thinly sliced
a tablespoon of black peppercorns, roughly crushed
4 spring onions
a round focaccia, not too thick
6 large slices of Parma ham (or San Daniele or coppa), thinly sliced
2 tablespoons (or so) finely grated Parmesan

Cut the mozzarella into thin slices and put it in a shallow dish. Cover it with the olive oil, the basil leaves, torn up a little, and the red chillies. Scatter the black peppercorns over the cheese. Cover with clingfilm and leave it to marinate. Half an hour will be enough, but leave it longer if you can. Meanwhile, grill the spring onions till lightly blackened in patches. They should be quite limp.

Halve the focaccia horizontally, hold the cheese in place in its dish and pour the marinating oil and milky juices over the cut sides of the bread. Cover the bottom half with the ham, then the mozzarella and bits, then the grilled onions, then finally the grated Parmesan. It will look rather beautiful at this point, like a piece of modern art. But if not, it's your lunch, so put the top half on and press gently, then lift it carefully on to a hot ridged griddle pan or a preheated baking sheet.

Either cook it on the hot griddle till the cheese starts to melt, turning once with the help of a wide, flat kitchen slice or bake it in an oven preheated to 180°C/Gas 4 for twenty to twenty-five minutes. The point is to get the outside toasted and the cheese oozing.

Cut into wedges and eat while the cheese is still molten and stringy.

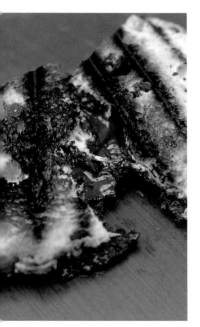

I am not sure you need the very darkest chocolate for this. Something with around 30–40 per cent cocoa butter is probably about right. You could, I think, eat this as a pudding by accompanying it with a dollop of ice-cream or softly whipped cream.

Makes 2

75g good-quality plain chocolate
4 thin slices cut downwards from a shallow panettone

Shave the chocolate using a vegetable peeler and divide between two of the pieces of panettone. Put the remaining slices on top and press down gently.

Heat a griddle pan – a frying pan will do – until it is moderately hot. If it gets too hot the bread will burn before the chocolate has melted. Place the sandwiches flat on the griddle and press down gently with a palette knife. Cook until the underside of the panettone is colouring slightly, then carefully turn and cook the other side. As soon as the chocolate has melted the sandwich is ready.

CHOCOLATE AND VANILLA
ICE-CREAM CROISSANTS

Enough for 4 as a snack

4 light and flaky croissants
8 small balls of vanilla ice-cream
the Sweet, Shiny Chocolate Sundae Sauce on page 288

Split the croissants in half horizontally and warm them under a grill or in the oven. Place the ice-cream on the bottom halves, then drizzle over the warm chocolate sauce and cover with the remaining halves of croissant.

Summer Berry Mascarpone Sandwich

Makes 4

strawberries, red and white currants, loganberries, tayberries,
  raspberries, apricots or plums
4 thin slices of panettone
6 heaped tablespoons mascarpone
a little vanilla extract

Remove the berries and currants from their stalks, stone the plums and apricots.

Toast the panettone briefly on both sides. It should be only slightly golden and still moist.

Flavour the cheese with a few drops of vanilla extract, stirring gently so as not to make the mascarpone too liquid. Spread on to the toasted panettone. Arrange the fruit loosely on top.

CHEESE

'I can only think of one or two things that are sexier in the mouth than crisp, flaky pastry and hot, flowing cheese (and one of those is an oyster) ...'

MELTING CHEESE

Camembert Baked in the Box
Baked Cheese-Filled Vine Leaves
Rarebit Puffs
Baked Goat's Cheese in Pastry
Goat's Cheese Tarts

CHEESE SOUPS AND SNACKS

Cauliflower Cheese and Mustard Soup
Leek and Blue Cheese Soup
Grilled Oysters with Cream and Parmesan
Peter Gordon's Mascarpone, Gorgonzola and
Poached Pear Salad

CHEESE SUPPERS

Potato Cakes with Pancetta and Cheese
Baked Plaice with Parmesan Crumbs
Pasta with Four Cheeses
Leek and Taleggio Risotto
Gruyère and Tarragon Soufflé
Roquefort and Mushroom Pancakes
Rowley Leigh's Cauliflower and Ricotta Salad with
Radishes, Olives, Parsley and Lemon
Alastair Little's Ricotta e Spinaci Rotolo

CHEESE PUDDINGS

Grilled Plums with Blackberries, Mascarpone
and Brown Sugar
Nigella Lawson's New York Cheesecake
Baked Lemon and Vanilla Cheesecake
Fruit Crumble Cheesecake

MELTING CHEESE

Cheese should melt rather than cook. The point of heating cheese is not to render it tender, like meat or fish or vegetables, but simply to allow it to soften and ooze. When we overcook cheese it turns oily and salty, as anyone who has ever mistimed a pizza will know. The point is simply to get it to become semi-liquid.

It is very easy to overcook cheese, which is why it is generally encased in pastry or cooked so swiftly that there is no time for it to do anything other than soften. It is this brief, protected cooking that makes it so enticing. Could anything be more pleasing in the mouth than a mixture of flaking, buttery puff pastry and hot, flowing cheese?

Some cheeses melt more sensuously than others. Ripe Camembert and Brie and gorgonzola are half-way there already. Fontina and Gruyère become less liquid than the others, while mozzarella forms strings that are fun to grapple with (unless you have a beard). Goat's cheeses are capricious. Sometimes they soften nicely, other times they become flaccid and grainy. The mature French ones are often the most successful. I wrap them in layers of puff or filo pastry to protect them from the heat and to provide the most gratifying contrast of texture. I can think of few sexier things to have in my mouth.

More than Cheddar

I cannot remember a day without cheese. It may be a pure, white, fresh *chèvre*; a narrow wedge of oozing Brie or a jagged lump of Montgomery's Cheddar. It could be the merest morsel of salty, pungent Roquefort or a snow-white lump of feta from the local Greek grocer. It may be one of those days when I try something new, like the mild and milky asiago I bought yesterday or perhaps an old favourite such as Cotherstone. Few bits of shopping excite me more than walking into my local cheese shop to see what takes my fancy. Sometimes I can hardly wait to get home to unwrap the waxed paper parcels.

I am lucky in having a wonderful cheese shop, Patricia Michelson's La Fromagerie in Highbury, North London, within a short walk of where I live. I buy elsewhere, too, unable to pass by a display of good cheese in the same way others cannot pass an antique shop or a department store, yet I rarely have much cheese in the house. I prefer one, or possibly two, truly fine pieces of cheese on the table to a groaning cheeseboard. One or two really good cheeses – perhaps a log of fudgy goat's cheese and a wedge of melting gorgonzola – are more enticing to me than lots of little bits on a board.

I cook with it, too. There is always a lump of Parmesan in my fridge – green salad with a mustardy dressing and lots of finely grated Parmesan is a staple lunch when I am working – and I would feel as lost without it as if I had no mineral water, olive oil or wine in the house. A little plastic-wrapped slab of feta has saved me more than once. But there is more to it than that. Sometimes I cook sliced potatoes slowly with taleggio, or grate Gruyère into a soufflé. A little piece of hard cheese may be grated finely into a salad; a creamy, wrinkle-rinded Saint-Marcellin may end up baked inside a vine leaf; pale, waxy fontina may well find itself inside a toasted sandwich.

I no more believe in cooking with those flavourless blocks of factory-produced cheese than I do in making a chocolate mousse with chocolate-flavoured cake covering or an ice-cream sundae with one of those products made from sugar and vegetable fat instead of cream, sugar and eggs. I believe passionately that what you get out depends on what you put in.

Camembert Baked in the Box

Pure indulgence, this. As the Camembert bakes, the cheese underneath the crust becomes a hot, creamy, sticky, smelly, bubbling pool.

Enough for 2

a whole small Camembert in its wooden box
a clove of garlic, peeled and halved
a little white wine

To serve:
new potatoes
gherkins

Take the cheese from its wooden box and remove the paper wrapping. Push the cheese back into the box.

Smear the top of the cheese with the cut halves of garlic. They will lightly scent the cheese without overpowering it (it is actually quite difficult to overpower a Camembert). Make half a dozen tiny holes in the rind and drizzle a little white wine into them. Just a few drops. Replace the lid. Bake in an oven preheated to 200°C/Gas 6 for twenty-five to thirty minutes or until hot and bubbling.

While the cheese is cooking, put the potatoes on to boil in salted water. Serve the melted cheese in its box, dipping in the spuds or some gherkins, or simply a chunk or two of very crusty bread.

BAKED CHEESE-FILLED VINE LEAVES

Another way of baking cheese in the oven till it bursts its skin and oozes all over the place. This time vine leaves just about manage to stop the hot, almost liquid, cheese escaping. You will need a lovely floury, crusty loaf to scoop up the bubbling *fromage*. Any small, lightly crusted cheese is suitable but I have had the most success with Saint-Marcellin and little *crottins*. I get my fresh vine leaves from the Greek grocer's shops scattered around North London; during winter they can be bought in brine, in which case they will need a thorough soaking before you use them.

Serves 6 as a snack or savoury

6 large, tender vine leaves
6 small, creamy cheeses
olive oil
crusty bread, to serve

Rinse the leaves, especially if you are not sure where they were grown. Bring a large pot of water to the boil and dunk the leaves in it for two minutes or until they become supple. Shake them dry. Place each leaf flat on the table and place a cheese in the centre. Fold the leaf over the cheese and secure with a cocktail stick or raffia. Place them seam-side up in an ovenproof dish. Drizzle over a little olive oil, just enough to moisten the leaves and form a shallow puddle in the bottom of the dish.

Bake in an oven preheated to 200°C/Gas 6 for about twelve to fifteen minutes or until the cheese has started to soften and ooze and the leaves are lightly crisp on top. Serve straight away, with crusty bread to mop up the melting cheese.

Rarebit Puffs

Welsh rarebit, rabbit or whatever, is one of the greatest things of all time – hot, mustardy, melting cheese and crisp toast. This recipe goes one better by replacing the toast with puff pastry and the usual cheese with a mixture of mascarpone and Parmesan, to give the most delectable little parcels.

Makes 12, enough for 4

30g butter
6 cloves of garlic, peeled and thinly sliced
7–8 tablespoons mascarpone
4 heaped tablespoons finely grated Parmesan
2 teaspoons made English mustard
375g chilled ready-rolled puff pastry
1 free range egg, beaten

Make the filling: melt the butter in a shallow pan, add the garlic and cook over a moderate heat, stirring from time to time, until it is soft and pale gold in colour. Tip the garlic and butter into a bowl and leave to cool. When it is no longer hot enough to melt the mascarpone, mix with the cheeses (saving one tablespoon of Parmesan for later) and the mustard and season with salt and pepper. Set aside.

Unroll the pastry and lay it out flat. Cut the pastry in four lengthways, then cut each piece into six equal pieces.

Put a heaped teaspoon of the mixture on twelve of the squares, dampen the edges with the beaten egg (milk or water will not seal them tightly enough), then lay a second square on top of each. Press tightly round the edges to seal; if any filling escapes just poke it back in and wipe the pastry edges. It is essential that they are sealed well otherwise the filling will ooze out during cooking. Transfer to a baking sheet, brush with beaten egg and scatter over the remaining Parmesan.

Bake in an oven preheated to 220°C/Gas 7 for ten to fifteen minutes, till puffed and golden. Serve immediately.

BAKED GOAT'S CHEESE IN PASTRY

Pesto works well here because of the affinity between basil and mild, chalky goat's cheese, but green or black olive paste or anchovy fillets roughly mashed with a little fruity extra virgin olive oil are possibilities too.

Serves 4

2 sheets of ready-rolled puff pastry, 20 x 18cm each
4 slices of goat's cheese, about 2.5cm thick or 4 individual cheeses, about 70g each
4 heaped tablespoons basil pesto
1 free range egg, beaten
2 tablespoons grated Parmesan

Cut each sheet of pastry in half and roll out lightly on a floured board to give four 18cm squares. Put one piece of cheese in the middle of each piece of pastry. Spoon over the pesto. Brush the edges of the pastry with some of the beaten egg. Bring the corners of the pastry up into the middle, pressing the edges together to seal. Alternatively, wrap them as if you were wrapping a parcel. Make sure they are firmly sealed.

Put the parcels on a baking sheet, brush with beaten egg and scatter over the Parmesan. Bake for fifteen to twenty minutes in an oven preheated to 200°C/Gas 6, until the pastry is pale gold and the cheese within is oozing.

Goat's Cheese Tarts

Crisp, flaking pastry, oozing goat's cheese.

Makes 6

375g ready-rolled puff pastry, thawed if necessary
3 soft, barrel-shaped goat's cheeses, or 2 goat's cheese logs
1 free range egg, beaten
a few sprigs of thyme or rosemary

Cut the pastry into six equal pieces, rolling each into a 13cm square.

Cut each cheese in half, or into three 5cm pieces if you are using logs. Place each piece of cheese on a square of pastry. Brush the edges of the pastry with beaten egg. Draw the sides of the pastry up to form a pyramid. Press the pastry edges together half-way up the sides, leaving the centre open. Add a small sprig of herb to each one.

Slide on to a baking sheet and bake in an oven preheated to 220°C/Gas 7 for fifteen minutes or until the pastry is golden and puffed up and the cheese has softened. Eat while the cheese is still warm.

POTATO CAKES WITH PANCETTA AND CHEESE

Enough for 3 as a light supper or lunch

100g thinly sliced pancetta
850g leftover boiled potatoes
25g butter
a tablespoon of olive oil
100g fontina, Gruyère or other easy-melting cheese, sliced

Fry the slices of pancetta in a shallow pan (make it a large one, then you can use it for the potato cakes afterwards) until their fat turns golden. Remove and set aside.

Grate the potatoes on the coarse side of the grater. This is much easier if they are cool. Season them with salt and pepper and squash the grated potato into flat patties, about as big as the palm of your hand. You should end up with about six.

Melt the butter with the olive oil in the pan. All the better if it is non-stick. When the butter starts to fizz, slide in three of the potato cakes with the aid of a slotted metal slice. Take care – they may spit. Cook over a moderate heat until they are golden underneath, then flip them carefully over (they may break but no matter) and continue to cook until they are golden on both sides and heated right through. Lift them out and keep warm while you cook the remaining cakes.

Return the cooked cakes to the pan; they should just fit tightly but if not then you may have to do them in two batches. Divide the cooked pancetta between the cakes, then lay the slices of cheese on top. Cover the pan with a lid and continue to cook for a couple of minutes, until the cheese has melted. Serve immediately.

BAKED PLAICE WITH PARMESAN CRUMBS

So worked up about cod and monkfish are we that the poor old plaice is often dismissed out of hand. Bought fresh, and I mean really fresh, a flat fillet of plaice is worth eating, but its flavour diminishes quickly. I am rather partial to a plaice – there is something peaceful about this fish. It is a gentle supper. I would not normally suggest a marriage of fish and cheese, yet the combination of plaice, white breadcrumbs and Parmesan is really rather good, and I urge you to try it.

Serves 2

2 large plaice fillets, skin on
4 gently heaping tablespoons fine, white fresh breadcrumbs
6 level tablespoons finely grated Parmesan
4 tablespoons melted butter
2 tablespoons olive oil

Lay the fish skin-side down in an ovenproof dish. Mix the breadcrumbs, cheese, melted butter and oil and grind over a little salt and black pepper. Spread the seasoned crumbs loosely over the fish, then bake for twenty minutes in an oven preheated to 220°C/Gas 7.

PASTA WITH FOUR CHEESES

Follow this with a bitter-leaf salad (try chicory, watercress and frisée) to contrast with the pasta's rib-sticking creaminess and to mop up the remains of the cheese sauce from your plate.

Serves 4

500g dried tube or shell pasta
60g butter
50g Gruyère, grated
50g fontina, diced
50g gorgonzola, diced
60g Parmesan, finely grated
90ml double cream

Bring a large, deep pan of water to the boil, salt it generously and drop in the pasta. When it returns to the boil, turn down the heat a little so that it does not boil over and cook at a fierce bubble until the pasta is tender but still firm between the teeth – about nine minutes for most dried pasta. Drain lightly, then return it to the pan with the butter.

Toss the hot pasta and the butter till the pasta is shining with melted butter, then add the four cheeses and a moderate seasoning of salt and black pepper. Remember that the cheeses themselves are quite salty. Mix the cheese into the pasta lightly with the cream, then tip into a large shallow dish. Put in an oven preheated to 200°C/Gas 6 until the cheese melts, about seven to ten minutes.

LEEK AND TALEGGIO RISOTTO

I am rather fond of risotto and its soothing texture. The addition of a cheese such as taleggio or Camembert makes it the most gently restoring of all suppers.

Serves 2 generously

50g butter
2 large leeks, chopped and rinsed
2 large cloves of garlic, peeled and sliced
a little dried oregano
225g arborio rice
900ml hot vegetable or chicken stock
225g taleggio or other soft, creamy cheese such Camembert, cut into
   thick slices

Put the butter into a shallow, heavy-bottomed pan and add the leeks and garlic. Cook over a moderate heat, stirring occasionally, until the leeks are soft. Don't hurry this; let the leeks cook slowly for about fifteen to twenty minutes, but stop cooking before they colour.

Stir in the oregano, a teaspoon or so will do, and the rice. Pour in three ladles of hot stock and stir. Leave to simmer gently, stirring regularly, until the stock has almost all been soaked up by the rice. Add more stock and leave to cook once more, at a gentle pace, then add more when that too has gone. It will stick if you forget to stir it. The rice will be plump and tender after about eighteen to twenty minutes. Taste it to see if it is done to your liking; it should have a bit of bite left in it but should be quite tender.

Stir in the cheese at the last minute – it will melt creamily. Check for seasoning; it will need both salt and black pepper.

GRUYÈRE AND TARRAGON SOUFFLÉ

Anyone can make a soufflé. A light hand when folding in the egg whites and a mild air of confidence are all you need to make this light and creamy soufflé that will wobble delightfully on the plate.

Serves 4 as a light supper

a little finely grated Parmesan for lining the dish
300ml milk
a bay leaf or two
50g butter, plus a little extra
50g plain flour
5 free range eggs, separated
a teaspoon of Dijon mustard
2 tablespoons tarragon leaves, chopped
100g Gruyère, grated

Brush the inside of a 1.5 litre soufflé dish with butter and sprinkle it with grated Parmesan. Shake out any excess cheese. Bring the milk to the boil with the bay leaf, then set aside. Melt the butter in a medium-sized, heavy-based saucepan and stir in the flour. Cook for a couple of minutes, until the mixture turns a deep ivory colour. Pour in the milk, stirring or whisking until you have a smooth sauce. Simmer gently, stirring from time to time, for about ten minutes.

Remove the sauce from the heat and take out the bay leaf. Stir the yolks into the sauce. Season with the mustard, tarragon, and some salt and ground black pepper. Stir in the Gruyère.

Beat the egg whites till thick and frothy and almost stiff. Fold them into the cheese sauce gently but thoroughly. A large metal spoon is the best tool for this. Scoop the mixture gently into the buttered soufflé dish and bake in an oven preheated to 200°C/Gas 6 for about twenty-five to thirty minutes, till the soufflé has risen and is golden on top. The outside should be crisp and the inside creamy and barely set.

ROQUEFORT AND MUSHROOM PANCAKES

This is not a dish to make in a hurry. If the weather is dull at the weekend I might spend an hour or so making it rather than trying to attempt it on a weekday evening. You need to be a little organized about things here. I know making pancakes is a bit of a fiddle but I think the end result is worth every little bit of effort.

For a dish such as this, where the béchamel sauce is just a small part, I suggest you buy it ready-made. Italian grocers and some supermarkets stock 500ml tetra packs of it under the name Chef Besciamella. Such commercial time-savers are fine for recipes like this, although if it were a major part of the dish, such as for cauliflower cheese, then I think it worth making your own.

ROQUEFORT AND MUSHROOM PANCAKES

Continued

Enough for 4

50g (a thick slice) butter
a large onion, peeled and chopped
2 large cloves of garlic, peeled and thinly sliced
300g small brown mushrooms
2 tablespoons chopped parsley
a teaspoon of dried oregano
50ml Madeira
250ml béchamel sauce, see page 225
100g Roquefort
75ml double or whipping cream
grated Parmesan

For the pancakes:
50g butter, plus more for cooking
100g plain flour
1 large free range egg
1 large egg yolk
350ml milk

For the pancakes, melt 50g of butter in a small pan and leave it to cool slightly. Sift the flour into a large mixing bowl with a good pinch of salt. Scoop a well into the centre of the flour, then drop in the egg and the egg yolk. Pour in the milk, whisking gently as you do, then whisk in the melted butter. Set the batter aside for about half an hour. Melt a little butter for frying the pancakes. Heat an 18–20cm crêpe pan, brush it with melted butter and pour in 50–60ml of batter (you had better give the batter a bit of a stir first; it should be the thickness of double cream).

The flat of the pan should just be covered in batter, but not thin enough to see through. Let the pancake cook until the underside is golden in patches and comes easily away from the pan. Lift one edge up with a palette knife and flip it gently over to cook the other side. It should be done in a minute, but will only colour in patches, not as evenly as the first side. Tip it carefully on to a plate. Brush the pan with more melted butter and continue until you have used all the batter.

For the filling, melt the butter in a deep saucepan and add the onion and garlic. Cook over a moderate heat until the onion becomes soft and pale gold. It should be tender to the touch and only lightly coloured. Meanwhile, chop the mushrooms finely. If they are particularly small, you can slice them thinly instead. Add the mushrooms to the onion, with a little more butter if the mixture seems dry, and let them cook until dark and soft, stirring to stop them sticking.

Stir in the herbs – you could add fresh or dried tarragon instead of the oregano if you prefer – then pour in the Madeira. Let it bubble, then leave for a minute or two until it is absorbed. Stir in the béchamel and crumble in the Roquefort. Season with black pepper and perhaps a little salt. Taste the mixture first; the Roquefort may have made it salty enough already. Let it cool a little.

Fill the pancakes with the mushroom mixture. I find this easiest one at a time: put a pancake, prettiest-side down, in a roasting or baking tin, spoon a dollop of the mushroom filling in the middle and fold over the edges. Push to the far end of the tin, then continue with the others, one at a time, until all are filled. Pour the cream around the edge of the tin, sprinkle with freshly grated Parmesan, then drizzle with any remaining melted butter. Bake in an oven preheated to 180°C/Gas 4 for twenty minutes, until the cheese is golden and the cream bubbling.

Rowley Leigh's Cauliflower & Ricotta Salad with Radishes, Olives, Parsley & Lemon

Anything this pretty must be good to eat. The cheese should preferably be *ricotta di bufala*, the by-product of the best mozzarella and more flavoursome than that made from cow's milk.

Serves 6

1 large cauliflower
50g black olives
2 spring onions
200g ricotta
200ml extra virgin olive oil
finely grated zest and strained juice of 3 lemons
1 egg yolk
$\frac{1}{2}$ teaspoon Dijon mustard
$\frac{1}{2}$ teaspoon sea salt
1 teaspoon coarsely ground black pepper
100g radishes, very finely sliced
the leaves of 2 sprigs of flat-leaf parsley

Carefully cut away the large florets with their stalks attached from the main stem of cauliflower. Cook them in plenty of boiling salted water for four to five minutes, keeping them slightly crunchy. Drain and leave to cool down in a colander. Halve the olives, removing the stones in the process.

Slice the spring onions very finely and mix well with the ricotta, a quarter of the olive oil and a little salt and pepper. Form the cheese mixture into a high mound in the middle of a serving plate. Wedge the cauliflower florets in the ricotta so as to re-form the shape of the original vegetable. Cover with a damp cloth if not serving immediately.

Put the lemon zest and juice, egg yolk, mustard, salt and pepper in a mixing bowl or blender. Whisk or blend in the remaining olive oil to make a smooth vinaigrette, adding a few drops of cold water if it gets too thick. Just before serving, pour this over the cauliflower and then scatter over the radishes, olives and parsley. Serve with crusty bread or grilled pitta bread.

ALASTAIR LITTLE'S RICOTTA E SPINACI ROTOLO

Alastair's elegant hot ricotta and spinach roll. Large sheets of fresh pasta can be bought from Italian delis that make pasta on the premises.

Serves 4-6

250g fresh spinach
250g good-quality ricotta
100g Parmesan, freshly grated
quarter of a nutmeg, freshly grated
a sheet of fresh pasta, approximately A3 size
400g tin of tomatoes
a clove of garlic, peeled and crushed
a pinch of sugar
a few basil leaves
good-quality olive oil

Check that the spinach is clean and remove any coarse stalks. Place it in a colander and slowly pour over a kettle of boiling water. Squeeze as much water as possible from the spinach. Chop the spinach roughly, using a knife. Please do this by hand to get the right consistency; a food processor will chop it too finely. Mix the spinach with the ricotta and Parmesan, breaking up the cheese. Season with the nutmeg and some salt and pepper. Spread this stuffing mixture over the pasta. Roll the pasta up into a long sausage and wrap it securely in foil, making sure it is watertight. Poach in water for about twenty minutes, then allow to cool in the water.

Make a very simple tomato sauce by cooking the tomatoes with the garlic, sugar, basil, a little olive oil and some salt and pepper until it has reduced to a saucelike consistency.

Remove the pasta roll from the poaching liquid and take off the foil. Cut the roll into slices about 2cm thick. Drizzle some oil into an ovenproof dish and lay the slices in the dish. Pour over the tomato sauce and another drizzle of olive oil and season. Put into a hot oven for five to ten minutes, until bubbling and heated through.

Sweet, White and Creamy

I sometimes think that the perfect dessert is one that includes a fresh, white, soft cheese and summer berries. (Then again, I also sometimes think that the perfect dessert is a steamed treacle sponge.) Peel back the cover of a tub of soft, creamy, fresh-tasting cheese such as mascarpone or ricotta or fromage frais and there lies a bland palette to play with. Vanilla, lemon zest, crystallized orange peel, scarlet fruits and chocolate all marry comfortably with ricotta, curd cheeses, the freshest sheep's cheeses and thick, unctuous mascarpone.

Turn a Petit Suisse out of its diminutive carton, pour over a puddle of thick yellow cream and scatter over a few mulberries and you have the dessert of my dreams, but sometimes we want something sweeter. The most famous cheese pudding is the cheesecake. A mile-high wedge of New York-style cheesecake takes some beating but I also like the fudgy, 'claggy'-textured 'yellow' cheesecakes with their undercarriage of sweet crumbs. Few turn down the offer.

Peaches, apricots and plums – swollen and ripe – can be stuffed with any cream cheese and grilled till it melts. A seasoning of cake or biscuit crumbs, chopped almonds or hazelnuts adds a welcome crunch. Or simply open a tub of mascarpone – the sexiest of all the cream cheeses – and dip in a teaspoon.

GRILLED PLUMS WITH BLACKBERRIES, MASCARPONE AND BROWN SUGAR

The plums must be ripe, by which I mean soft and heavy with juice. Should they not be as ripe as they could be, I suggest you bake them instead of grilling, giving them time to soften in the heat.

Serves 4

6 large, ripe plums
12 blackberries
a few drops of brandy or kirsch
a few drops of vanilla extract
12 heaped tablespoons mascarpone
6 heaped tablespoons demerara sugar

Cut the plums in half and remove and discard the stones. Place the plums cut-side up in a shallow baking dish. Pop a fat, juicy blackberry into each hollow. Mix the brandy or kirsch and vanilla extract with the mascarpone and spoon it on to the plums. Some will inevitably run off as they cook, but no matter. Sprinkle with the sugar and grill till it caramelizes – a matter of a couple of minutes under a thoroughly preheated grill.

Nigella Lawson's New York Cheesecake

A truly superb cheesecake, deep and not too sweet.

Serves 12

250g digestive biscuits, crushed to fine crumbs
150g butter, melted
225g plus 3 tablespoons caster sugar
2 tablespoons cornflour
750g full fat soft cream cheese
6 free range eggs, separated
2 teaspoons vanilla extract
150ml double cream
150ml soured cream
$\frac{1}{2}$ teaspoon salt
grated zest of 1 lemon
icing sugar or vanilla sugar for dusting

Butter the bottom and sides of a 24cm springform cake tin. Mix together the crushed biscuits, melted butter and 3 tablespoons of sugar and press on to the base of the tin. Chill for one hour.

In a large bowl, mix together the remaining sugar and the cornflour. Beat in the cream cheese, egg yolks and vanilla, either by hand or with an electric beater, then slowly pour in both creams, beating constantly. Add the salt and lemon zest.

Whisk the egg whites to stiff peaks, then fold into the cheese mixture. Scoop on to the chilled base. Bake in an oven preheated to 170°C/Gas 3 for one to one and a half hours without opening the oven door, until the cheesecake is golden brown on top. Turn off the heat and let the cake stand in the oven for two more hours. Then open the oven door and let it stand for a further hour. Serve chilled, dusted with icing sugar or vanilla sugar.

BAKED LEMON AND VANILLA CHEESECAKE

A fudgy vanilla cheesecake that is much better for a night in the fridge. You will need a deep 23cm cake tin with a removable base.

Serves 8–10

250g digestive biscuits
90g butter, melted
500g full-fat curd cheese or mascarpone
250g caster sugar
3 free range eggs, beaten
165ml double cream
the zest and juice of a lemon
a few drops of vanilla extract
200ml soured cream

Smash the digestive biscuits to crumbs in a food processor or put them in a plastic bag and roll them with a rolling pin. Mix them with the melted butter, then tip them into the cake tin. Press the warm, wet crumbs down with your hand to form a base, then set aside in a cool place.

Beat the curd cheese or mascarpone with the sugar until thick and creamy, then beat in the eggs. Pour in the cream – the beater still on a slow speed – then add the lemon zest and juice and a few drops of vanilla extract.

Pour the mixture on top of the crumbs and place in an oven preheated to 150°C/Gas 2 for an hour and a quarter, by which time the cake should be risen and starting to pucker round the edges. The centre should be wobbly but not runny. Switch off the oven but leave the cake in for fifteen minutes, then remove and leave in a cool place till it has sunk slightly and is thoroughly cool. It should be refrigerated overnight before eating if you get the chance. Just before serving, spread cold soured cream over the surface.

FRUIT CRUMBLE CHEESECAKE

Serves 6

150g digestive or Nice biscuits
50g butter, melted
450g full-fat curd cheese
2 free range eggs, beaten
zest of a lemon
175g caster sugar
300g assorted currants and blackberries, stalks removed

For the topping:
100g plain flour
75g butter
50g caster sugar

Crush the biscuits in a food processor or put them in a plastic bag and roll them with a rolling pin. Mix with the melted butter and tip into a 20–22cm loose-bottomed tart tin or shallow cake tin. Press the warm, wet crumbs down with your hand to form a base, then put in the fridge.

Mix the curd cheese, beaten eggs, lemon zest and half the sugar with a hand-held electric mixer. It should be thick and creamy. Put the tart tin on a baking sheet. Pour the filling into the crust and bake in an oven preheated to 180°C/Gas 4 for forty to forty-five minutes or until almost set. Meanwhile, put the prepared fruit in a pan with the remaining sugar and a tablespoon of water. Bring to the boil over a moderate heat and simmer until the blackcurrants just start to burst. Set aside to cool a little. For the topping, whizz the flour, butter and caster sugar in a food processor until they resemble breadcrumbs.

Remove the cheesecake from the oven and let it cool slightly. Lift the fruit from its juice with a draining spoon and spoon over the top of the cheesecake. Pour over a tablespoon of the juice, then chill the rest. Scatter the crumble mixture over the fruit and return the cheesecake to the oven for twenty to twenty-five minutes or until the crumble is starting to colour. Remove from the oven and leave in a cool place. Serve the cheesecake with the juices from the fruits.

ICE-CREAM

'Balls of vanilla or strawberry ice came in dented silver dishes, with a wafer shaped like a fan. I used to lick up every last, tiny drop of the melted puddle in the bottom and catch the little beads of condensation that ran down the outside of the dish with my finger, watching them join up into little rivulets.'

HOME-MADE ICES

An Old-Fashioned Milky Vanilla Ice

Banana Ice-Cream with Brandy Snap Wafers

Lemon and Sheep's Yoghurt Ice-Cream

Nigella Lawson's Fig Ice-Cream

Peter Gordon's Tamarind Ice-Cream

Lime Mascarpone Sorbet

Pink Grapefruit Sorbet

Summer Pudding Crème Fraîche Sorbet

ICE-CREAM SUNDAES

Raspberry Chocolate Sundae

Affogato al Caffé

HOT ICE-CREAM PUDDINGS

Hot Ice-Cream Pudding

Deep-Fried Ice-Cream and Mincemeat Parcels

Croissants with Caramelized Apples
and Caramel Ice-Cream

FRUIT, CREAM, EGGS, SUGAR ... AND NOSTALGIA

There is something magical about ices. The most minute spoonful can evoke a memory so clearly. That tiny, expensive *sorbetto di limone* at a grand, flaking bar in Venice; a lick of an ice-cream wafer at the English seaside; the melting pistachio ices in the heat of Athens in summer; the long, furrowed whirl of a Mr Whippy from a van; or a gelatinous, marshmallow-textured saffron ice from a Lebanese grocery. Or the *semi-freddo* I ate at midnight, sitting on the pavement in Florence, long ago and hopelessly in love.

Perhaps my passion for ices is partly a nostalgia thing. Or perhaps I just crave the tingle of a mango sorbet on my tongue or the snap of thin chocolate on a choc-ice. Or could it be that a tub of ice-cream is something I can eat without taking my eyes off the television screen? Whatever, ice-cream is a passion, whether it is the ones I make at home in the freezer compartment of my fridge from fresh eggs, thick cream and ripe fruit, or a deep, thick glass full of a spectacularly vulgar sundae, or just the tiniest spoonful of vanilla ice with my espresso.

LEMON AND SHEEP'S YOGHURT ICE-CREAM

A delightfully light and refreshing, creamy yellow ice. It can be made in an electric ice-cream machine, in which case it will be particularly light, or simply frozen. It works well enough in the ice-making compartment in the top of the fridge too, especially if you take it out during freezing to beat it. Sheep's milk yoghurt is not as exotic as it sounds – it can be bought in healthfood shops.

Enough for 6

600ml double cream
5 free range egg yolks
200g golden caster sugar
450g sheep's milk yoghurt
juice and zest of 3 large, juicy lemons

Put the cream in a heavy-based saucepan and bring almost to boiling point. Remove from the heat and set aside. Whisk the egg yolks and sugar in an electric mixer till fluffy. Pour in the warm cream and continue mixing. Now rinse the saucepan in which you heated the cream and pour the mixture into it. Place over a low heat, stirring constantly and making certain to get to the corners of the pan, until it has thickened to the consistency of double cream. Take great care it doesn't 'catch' and burn. A good test to see if it is ready is to run your finger along the back of the stirring spoon; if it leaves a clear line, then the custard is ready. Pour through a sieve into a large basin and leave to cool.

Now stir the sheep's yoghurt into the custard, then pour it back into the bowl of the electric mixer. Put it on low speed, then slowly pour in the lemon juice and zest. Pour either into a prepared electric ice-cream churn and follow your manufacturer's instructions or into a shallow metal or plastic container and put in the freezer for two hours. Remove, beat the frozen edges into the softer middle, then return to the freezer and leave till frozen.

LIME MASCARPONE SORBET

Serves 4–6

750ml water
350g golden caster sugar
the juice and finely grated zest of 5 limes
250g mascarpone

Put the water and sugar in a saucepan and bring to the boil. Stir in the lime zest and set aside to cool. Now stir in the juice and the mascarpone. Scrape into a metal or plastic container and put in the freezer or an ice-cream machine.

If you are using a freezer, remove the sorbet after two hours and beat it firmly, bringing the frozen edges into the middle. Now return it to the freezer for a further hour, repeat, then freeze again. At this point you might well wonder what on earth I am up to as the mixture will look somewhat dodgy, with a frozen layer of white on top and a liquid layer underneath. Trust me. It will all blend together at the final beating. When the mixture is well on its way to being frozen (the length of time this will take depends entirely on your freezer but it will probably be a good couple of hours) you must take it out and beat it again. Move the sorbet to the fridge fifteen to twenty minutes before you intend to serve it.

PINK GRAPEFRUIT SORBET

Serves 4–6

250g golden caster sugar
250ml water
3 pink grapefruits, preferably organic
the juice of 2 lemons

Put the sugar and water in a saucepan and bring to the boil. Once the sugar has dissolved, remove from the heat.

Unless the grapefruits are organically grown you will have to give them a really good wash to remove the wax the producers put on them to preserve them. Remove the zest with a lemon zester. Try not to get any of the bitter white pith underneath the zest. Put the zest into the sugar syrup and simmer for about ten minutes, until the zest is soft. Set aside to cool. Squeeze the grapefruits and the lemons and mix the juice with the cold grapefruit syrup. Now either pour the syrup into an ice-cream machine and follow the manufacturer's instructions or pour it into a shallow dish and freeze in the freezer or in the ice compartment at the top of the fridge. After two hours in the freezer it will need a good beating, preferably with a small electric whisk, bringing the frozen edges into the middle. Then again an hour later. It should be frozen in about five or six hours, depending on your freezer.

SUMMER PUDDING CRÈME FRAÎCHE SORBET

An ice of the most intense colour and flavour, best made in a sorbetière. It is not for the faint-hearted.

Serves 4

250g blackcurrants
250g redcurrants
250g raspberries
100g blackberries
225g golden caster sugar
100ml crème fraîche

Put the fruit into a stainless-steel saucepan with the sugar and a tablespoon of water. Heat gently, till the skins start to burst and the juices run a rich purple-red. Allow to cool.

Push the fruit through a sieve, pressing hard with the back of a spoon to get all the juice and flesh from the fruit. You will be left with a dry pulp and stalks. Either pour into an electric ice-cream churn and follow the manufacturer's instructions, adding the crème fraîche once the mixture has just started to freeze, or pour into a shallow metal or plastic container and place in the freezer or the ice compartment of a fridge. Remove after two hours and beat in the crème fraîche, preferably with a small hand-held electric beater (or put it in the blender), then return to the freezer. It should be ready after a total freezing time of four or five hours.

RASPBERRY CHOCOLATE SUNDAE

Fine chocolate, ripe, heavily fragrant raspberries, the best vanilla ice-cream and crisp, freshly toasted almonds will lift this delightfully vulgar sundae to a higher level. The most suitable wafers are those thin, cigarette-style ones filled with chocolate. They are available from Italian delicatessens.

Makes 2

the Sweet, Shiny Chocolate Sundae Sauce on page 288
125g raspberries
4 large balls of vanilla ice-cream
a handful of flaked almonds, toasted
chocolate wafer biscuits

Make the sauce and let it cool slightly. Crush the raspberries lightly with a fork. Put a little of the chocolate sauce in the bottom of two sundae glasses. Drop in some of the crushed raspberries, the vanilla ice-cream, more raspberries and some of the chocolate sauce. Scatter with the toasted flaked almonds, then stick in the wafers.

AFFOGATO AL CAFFÉ

That I have included this here is an act of pure selfishness. It happens to be my favourite ice-cream dessert. The espresso must be very strong and fragrant, the vanilla ice the very best.

Serves 4

8 neat balls of very good-quality vanilla ice-cream
4 small cups of hot, freshly made espresso coffee
small almond biscuits, to serve

The ice-cream should be quite hard, but soft enough to scoop without breaking. Put two balls in each of four small china dishes. I think they should be white, don't you? Then pour over the hot espresso. Serve immediately. If not sooner.

HOT ICE-CREAM PUDDING

A shallow, creamy, sticky pudding made with ice-cream. Bizzare, but delicious, it tastes like a cross between trifle and treacle pudding – in other words, my idea of heaven. It will appeal to those with an extraordinarily sweet tooth. Make sure you use only the best ice-cream made with egg yolks, such as Rocombe Farm, otherwise the pudding will not set. Anything that includes vegetable fat in its list of ingredients will not work. The idea comes from the French cook, the late Mère Brazier, who thought it was a good use for leftover ice-cream. Who, I might ask, has ever heard of 'leftover ice-cream'? It is a good way of using up little bits of ice-cream you may have in the freezer.

Serves 2–4

150g golden caster sugar
500g good-quality vanilla ice-cream
150g sponge fingers or trifle sponges

Put the sugar in a saucepan and add just enough water to cover it. Bring to the boil, then watch it while it thickens and turns to caramel. Don't stir it, which would make it crystallize, just leave it to bubble until it starts to turn amber coloured.

As soon as the caramel turns a deep caramel brown, but before it turns black and starts to smoke, pour it carefully (it may splutter) into an ovenproof dish, about 1.5 litres capacity. Leave for a few minutes to set. Turn the ice-cream into a mixing bowl and mash it with the sponge fingers. It may melt a little, but don't crush the biscuits to a powder; they should stay in chunks. Pour the lumpy mess into the caramel-lined dish and place the dish carefully in a roasting tin. Pour enough hot water in the tin to come half-way up the side of the dish and bake in an oven preheated to 180°C/Gas 4 for about twenty to twenty-five minutes. It is ready when the top is pale and crisp and the underside still moist and creamy. Serve warm and, dare I say it, with some pouring cream on the side.

Deep-Fried Ice-Cream and Mincemeat Parcels

A splendidly decadent mixture of hot, crisp pastry, boozy mincemeat and cold vanilla ice. This is my version of cookery writer and restaurateur Ruth Watson's brilliant recipe. Apparently the Victorians did a similar thing and called it Alaska Pie.

Makes 12

250g pack of filo pastry, each sheet about 30 x 45cm
400g finest-quality mincemeat
500ml vanilla ice-cream
groundnut or vegetable oil for deep-frying
golden icing sugar for dusting

You will need only twelve of the sheets of filo. Place them in front of you on a clean, dry work surface or chopping board. The longer side should face you. Fold the first sheet in half, right over left, so that you are working with a double thickness. Turn the sheet of pastry clockwise so that the open edges are away from you, the folded edge nearest. Put a generous heaped tablespoon of mincemeat in the centre of the pastry, followed by a scoop of vanilla ice-cream.

Take the long, folded edge nearest you and place it over the ice-cream and mincemeat. Then fold in the right-hand side to the centre to overlap the other side, followed by the left-hand edge. Then turn the parcel over and away from you so that the pastry encloses the filling completely. Place on a metal tray and rush it to the freezer. Continue with the remaining pastry. Freeze for at least two hours (don't try to hurry the process) so that the ice-cream is really firm by the time you want to fry each parcel.

Heat the oil in a deep-fat fryer to 195°C. Lower the parcels, two at a time, in the frying basket. Each parcel will take two and a half minutes to cook. I know this sounds a little pedantic, but if you overcook them the ice-cream will melt and then you will have the most ghastly mess on your hands and never forgive me. The pastry should be pale gold. You may need to hold the parcels down with a palette knife – they have a tendency to bob around like buoys at sea. Drain on kitchen paper and pat the parcels gently to get rid of any excess oil. Dust with sifted icing sugar and eat straight away, whilst the pastry is still hot and crisp and the ice-cream is still cold.

CROISSANTS WITH CARAMELIZED APPLES AND CARAMEL ICE-CREAM

Serves 4 as a pudding or sweet snack (or, better still, a midnight feast)

50g butter
2 large dessert apples or 3 small ones
4 tablespoons golden caster sugar
a good slug of Calvados
4 small flaky croissants
caramel or almond ice-cream

Melt the butter in a shallow pan. Quarter and core the apples and cut each quarter into three or four segments. When the butter is hot, add the apples and cook them till golden and almost tender, turning once to cook the other side. Then add the sugar and Calvados and cook until the mixture starts to caramelize.

Split the croissants in half and toast under a hot grill for a minute or two until warm. Remove from the heat and put a couple of generous scoops of ice-cream on each bottom half, then spoon over the hot apples and their pan juices. Just as the ice-cream starts to melt, put on the top half of each croissant and eat straight away, while the apples are still hot.

SUCK IT AND SEE

Ice-cream, like fish and chips, always tastes better by the sea. I love the stuff – be it the modern banana-nut-crunch-super-chunk type sold in tubs at four quid a pop or a good old Mr Whippy from a smoke-belching van. It could be Rocombe Farm's Vanilla made with free range eggs and Jersey cream, Hill Station's Aromatic Cardamom, Green & Black's Organic Chocolate (a lovely old-fashioned flavour, that one) or a pot of Ben and Jerry's – it matters little.

As much as I admire the modern ice creams, even the super-sophisticated American ones, I miss the simpler stuff we used to eat as kids. What I really miss is the Raspberry Ripples and Pineapple Mivvies that came on a stick, the ice-lolly called Fab that had hundreds and thousands sprinkled on the end, and the original 99s. Do you remember how the chocolate flake was always slightly stale? I loved, too, the way the paper-thin chocolate snapped and crackled on a cheap choc-ice and those little tubs of ice-cream at the theatre that were always so hard you couldn't get your wooden spoon in. My teeth would tingle when they bit into the cold ice-cream and the funny, flat wooden spoon.

Best of all were the rather watery chocolate lollies on sticks and the cornet with ice-cream that you had to unwrap from its roll of cardboard. How I loved licking that cardboard.

I have now reached the age when I might enjoy a thick slice of vanilla ice-cream sandwiched between two wafers. The sort of boring thing my parents would eat when I was sucking a Zoom. One of the signs of getting old is that you start to like things such as ice-cream wafers. The best were the hand-made ice-creams from small dairies, most of which have long been put out of business by the 'big boys' or closed down because of the expense of meeting absurdly rigorous hygiene standards. This was the best ice-cream, thick and full of naughty little ice crystals.

The greatest treat of all was having an ice-cream at the café in the Winter Gardens overlooking the sea. Most of the resorts we went to had one. The sort of place that had clocks made out of flowers all along the front. The balls of vanilla or strawberry ice came in dented silver dishes, with a wafer shaped like a fan. Bliss. I used to lick up every last, tiny drop, then I would touch the little beads of condensation on the outside of the dish with my finger, watching then join up into rivulets.

Recently I have taken to making my own ices. It is not the first time. I used to have an ice-lolly mould when I was a kid and made orange lollies with round white sticks that went through tiny holes in the side of the mould. It is easy enough to make ice-cream and sorbets at home even without an ice-cream machine, but you have to keep beating them every hour as they freeze so that they do not set into one impenetrable block. An ice-cream machine is one of those things I worried would be a space-hogging toy that I used briefly then forgot about. In fact it is a joy beyond my wildest dreams.

I have been playing around with everything from crushed red-currants to vanilla custard and sheep's yoghurt to pink grapefruits. Yes, the machines are expensive, yes, they do take up heaps of space in a small kitchen like mine, but they produce ices of the most unbelievably intense flavour – so clear, bright and fresh – that I now regard a sorbetière as essential a piece of kitchen equipment for me as a vegetable peeler or a decent bread knife. But then, I am something of an ice-cream evangelist.

CHOCOLATE

'I sometimes think I could kill for a slice of chocolate cake; especially the shallow French ones that are all fudgy in the middle, or the sort we sell at village fêtes, sandwiched together with coffee buttercream.'

CHOCOLATE TRUFFLES

Chocolate Truffles

Chocolate-Coated Truffles

CHOCOLATE SAUCES

A Good Chocolate Sauce

A Sweet, Shiny Chocolate Sundae Sauce

Chocolate Toblerone Sauce

HOT CHOCOLATE PUDDINGS

Nigella Lawson's Sticky Chocolate Pudding

Hot Chocolate Pudding

Chocolate Apple Betty

Rowley Leigh's Hot Chocolate Soufflé

COLD CHOCOLATE PUDDINGS

Pears with Florentine Cream

White Chocolate Cardamom Mousse

CHOCOLATE CAKES

Chocolate Espresso Cake

No-Cook Chocolate Cake

Chocolate Cornflake Cakes

A WORLD WITHOUT CHOCOLATE?

How horrible it would be to live in a world without chocolate. A world devoid of the strings of sticky caramel in a Mars Bar; the crisp snap of a square of the finest Valrhona Manjari; the feel of a pale Flake as it dissolves on the tongue; and the hot-cold sensation of warm chocolate sauce on a cold vanilla ice.

I should hate to do without the occasional jagged piece of dark, bitter chocolate with an espresso or the rude pleasures of sticking my tongue down a Walnut Whip. And how could I survive without chocolate cake? A slice of the thinnest, darkest, wettest chocolate torte or a big fat wedge of a chocolate buttercream cake. A soft, fluffy roulade with a layer of snow-white cream or one of those shallow, gooey chef's cakes that come as a thin sliver on a big white plate.

Dark and velvety sauces; smooth, mild ice-creams; warming, soporific drinks and sugar-laden fudge. Chocolate runs through my life like a comfort blanket; a teddy bear you can eat. I can show off with boxes of truffles from the most expensive Parisian shops or devour a Toffee Crisp in absolute solitude. For all my banging on about the world's finest chocolate, I can still demolish a packet of Rolos in minutes. I simply love chocolate. I adore it. I want it.

CHOCOLATE: THE GOOD THE BAD AND THE EVEN BETTER

I think of chocolate as one of two types: fine chocolate and fun chocolate. Sometimes I want to eat chocolate that has been made from the finest cocoa beans, a large dose of expensive cocoa butter (the precious liquid that gives fine chocolate its character and flavour) and a little sugar. I want to unwrap it from its expensive designer paper and foil, snap it crisply from the bar and wait for it to melt slowly on my tongue. Fine chocolate breaks with a crisp snap.

Other times, I want the fun stuff. I want to hear the soft, dull thud of a bar of candy-style chocolate – one of the sugary-sweet chocolate bars so famous that their names have become part of our culture. Bars designed to give instant energy or simply to comfort. Low in cocoa butter and high in bland fat and sugar, they are sometimes just what I want. Comfort. That is what chocolate bars and cheap chocolate do; they comfort us with their sweet stickiness and coat our mouths with a layer of mild, chocolatey fat. Gorgeous.

Yet I cook only with fine chocolate. The best that money can buy. It is a question of flavour. For the deepest true chocolate flavour in a cake or pudding you need an ingredient with plenty of clout. This only comes from chocolate with a high cocoa butter content, by which I mean 60 or 70 per cent. This also means that it will melt smoothly and voluptuously. Fun chocolate (with one or two exceptions) melts erratically and cloys on the tongue, offering no depth of flavour in cake or pud.

CHOCOLATE TRUFFLES

I am convinced the best truffles are those made from nothing more than chocolate and cream. Some like to add a little butter, others a splash of brandy or fruit liqueur, but I remain loyal to the simplicity of the two-ingredient truffle. Neither do I think that rolling the truffle mix into perfect balls adds anything more than fingerprints. A craggy, free-form shape has charm enough.

The quality of the chocolate is crucial. It is the heart and soul of a truffle. The chocolate needs to have a deep flavour that will not be diluted by the bland cream. A high cocoa butter content will give a velvety texture and a clean finish in the mouth. Size is a matter of choice but I like a two-bite truffle. I like the way the chocolate then has just enough time to leave a thin layer of melted chocolate on your fingertips – something to lick discreetly after the truffle has gone.

CHOCOLATE TRUFFLES

Makes about 500g

450g fine chocolate
275ml whipping cream
cocoa powder for dusting

Chop the chocolate finely; the pieces should be about the same size as gravel. They will melt more successfully if they are all of roughly equal size. A large, heavy cook's knife will make the chopping easier than using a small one.

Put the chopped chocolate in a large heatproof bowl. If the bowl is warm it will help the chocolate to melt. Bring the cream to the boil in a small pan. Just as it reaches boiling point, remove from the heat and pour slowly into the chocolate, beating gently with a wooden spoon.

The chocolate should all melt into a thick, glossy, dark-brown cream. If there are lumps left, then you will have to put the bowl over a pan of hot, almost simmering, water until they melt. But take care not to overheat it, which will result in the mixture separating and curdling.

Place the basin of chocolate in the fridge to stiffen. Depending on the temperature inside your fridge, the mixture will need about an hour to thicken. (It should not set solid, although if it does, just melt it over hot water and refrigerate again.) Now you have a choice: thick, solid, luxurious truffles or softer, lighter ones. If you prefer, as I do, an unwhipped truffle with a rich texture, then leave the mix as it is. If you like a soft, airy truffle, beat the mixture with an electric whisk for a minute or so until it starts to change colour. It will become paler and fill with air. Overwhipping will curdle the truffle mixture.

Using two teaspoons, scoop out balls of truffle and drop them into the cocoa powder. The size is a matter of choice. I like a large truffle; others may prefer to make a smaller one that can be eaten in one go. Roll them lightly into rounds if you wish, though I prefer them as rough-textured lumps. Roll the truffles in the cocoa, then leave them in a cool place for an hour to set.

CHOCOLATE-COATED TRUFFLES

As delectable as the rich truffles in the preceding recipe are, they are even better when coated in a crisp, bitter chocolate shell. You can simply dip them into melted chocolate or temper the chocolate, as below. Taking the time to temper the chocolate will result in a glossier finish.

the truffles as before
375g fine plain chocolate
cocoa powder for dusting

Chop the chocolate finely and put about two-thirds of it into a large heatproof bowl. Balance the bowl comfortably over a large pan of hot water. The heat need not be on under the pan; I usually bring the water to the boil, then turn off the heat before placing the basin of chocolate on top. The bottom of the bowl should not touch the water, which will cause the chocolate to overheat. Resist the temptation to do anything but stir very occasionally and very gently.

If you have a kitchen thermometer, heat the chocolate until it reaches 48–55°C. If you have no thermometer, heat the chocolate until it is completely liquid, with no lumps of solid chocolate in it. Add the remaining chopped chocolate to the liquid chocolate. It will become partially solid. Leave it to melt over the hot water again.

Carefully lift each truffle with a couple of forks and dip into the liquid chocolate. Drop into the cocoa powder, roll very lightly and leave in a cool place to harden.

Chocolate Sauces

We want different chocolate sauces for different occasions. Something dark and serious for pouring over cold vanilla ice-cream, which will set instantly to a wafer-thin, crisp shell; a glossy, sticky sauce for pouring into an over-the-top ice-cream sundae or where you need the chocolate to stay liquid even when cold; and a milky, fudgy, nutty one for occasional moments of sheer gluttony.

A Good Chocolate Sauce

This is a luscious, not-too-sweet sauce suitable for pouring over poached pears, meringues and ice-cream. It is good natured provided it is not overheated or stirred too often.

250g fine plain chocolate
2 tablespoons strong black coffee (espresso is ideal)
300ml whipping cream
a knob of butter about the size of a walnut

Break the chocolate into small pieces so that it melts easily. Put it into a heavy-bottomed saucepan with the coffee and the cream. Heat slowly, stirring from time to time, until the chocolate has melted. It is essential that the heat is kept low. Once the chocolate is softened, stir until smooth, then stir in the butter and pour into a warm jug. Serve warm.

A Sweet, Shiny Chocolate Sundae Sauce

A dark, glossy sauce that does not set too quickly, making it perfect to layer amongst ice-cream in a sundae. Try pouring it over layers of coffee and vanilla ice-cream.

175g fine plain chocolate
50g butter
50g caster sugar
2 tablespoons golden syrup
200ml milk

Break the chocolate into squares and melt it, with the butter, in a bowl set over a pan of hot water. Stir in the sugar and syrup until dissolved, then pour in the milk and continue to cook, stirring often, until the sauce thickens.

CHOCOLATE TOBLERONE SAUCE

The joy of melting Toblerone rather than ordinary commercial chocolate bars is that it contains chopped praline, which leaves you with a wonderfully nutty sauce that is particularly good over vanilla ice-cream or pancakes. And, of course, saves you the task of making praline with sugar and almonds.

200g dark Toblerone
30g butter
100ml whipping cream

Break the Toblerone into triangles, then chop it finely. Melt it in a heatproof bowl set over a pan of simmering water. Don't be tempted to stir it too much; just leave it be until it is completely soft. Add the butter and stir until melted, then gently stir in the cream. The sauce is now ready to use.

Nigella Lawson's Sticky Chocolate Pudding

This is Nigella Lawson's version of one of those miraculous puddings that splits during cooking to give a sticky sponge on top and a gorgeous chocolate sauce underneath.

Serves 6

150g self-raising flour
25g good-quality cocoa powder
200g caster sugar
50g ground hazelnuts
75g dark chocolate buttons (or dark chocolate, chopped)
180ml full cream milk
1 teaspoon vanilla extract
40g butter, melted
1 free range egg

For the sauce:
180g dark muscovado sugar
120g good-quality cocoa powder, sifted
500ml very hot water

Put all the dry ingredients – the flour, cocoa, sugar, ground hazelnuts and chocolate pieces – in a large mixing bowl. Whisk together the milk, vanilla extract, melted butter and egg. Pour into the bowl containing the dry ingredients and mix thoroughly.

Pour the mixture into a large, buttered soufflé dish, about 20cm in diameter. Mix the muscovado sugar and cocoa together and sprinkle on top of the pudding. Pour the hot water on top – there is no need to stir – and put in an oven preheated to 180°C/Gas 4. After thirty-five to forty minutes the pudding should be firm and springy. Serve at once, with cold pouring cream.

Hot Chocolate Pudding

This could be described as a good-natured chocolate soufflé. You will need an 850ml ovenproof china dish – I use a deep, rectangular white china terrine.

Serves 4

150g fine dark chocolate
a little butter
75g caster sugar
4 large free range eggs, separated

Break the chocolate into small pieces and put it in a pudding basin in a large saucepan. Pour enough water into the pan to come half-way up the sides of the basin, then place over a moderate heat until the chocolate has melted. There is no need to stir at all, but you should check that the heat is turned very low or even off as soon as the chocolate starts to soften.

Meanwhile, rub a smidgeon of butter round the inside of the dish and sprinkle it with a very little of the measured sugar. Whisk the egg yolks and sugar together until they are pale and fluffy – I use one of those hand-held electric beaters. Wash the whisks and dry them carefully, then beat the egg whites in a separate bowl until thick and standing in peaks.

Working quickly but gently, fold the melted chocolate into the egg yolks and sugar (a rubber spatula will help here) and then fold in the beaten egg whites. Fold slowly and deeply so that you disperse the whites into the chocolate mixture but without losing any of the air. Overmixing will result in a flat pudding. Scoop the mixture into the prepared dish and bake for twenty-five minutes in an oven preheated to 200°C/Gas 6.

The pudding is done when it is spongy almost through to the centre, where it should still be very slightly creamy. Serve with double cream.

CHOCOLATE APPLE BETTY

An old-fashioned pudding with a discreet use of chocolate. What I particularly like about this pudding (even more than its absurdly easy method) is the contrast between fluffy, tart apple and sweet, crisp crumbs.

Serves 4, with cream or vanilla ice-cream

1kg Bramley apples, peeled and cored
30g butter

For the crumb layer:
125g soft white breadcrumbs
100g light soft brown sugar
100g dark chocolate, roughly chopped
75g butter, melted
3 heaped tablespoons golden syrup

Cut the apples into large chunks, put them in a pan and toss with the butter and a couple of tablespoons of water over a moderate heat. When the apples start to soften but are still keeping their shape, tip them into a 1.5 litre baking dish.

Mix the crumbs, sugar and chocolate and cover the apples loosely with the mixture. Melt the butter with the golden syrup in a small saucepan, then pour it over the crumbs, making certain to soak them all. Bake in an oven preheated to 190°C/Gas 5 for thirty-five minutes, till the apple is soft and the crumbs are golden and crisp.

Rowley Leigh's Hot Chocolate Soufflé

Utter bliss from Rowley Leigh. The marriage of chocolate and pistachio – especially in this case when the chocolate is hot and the pistachio cold – is one made in heaven. As he says, 'I first came across this combination in Paris. My boss, Albert Roux, had taken me to dinner at Lucas Carton and during the meal I was aware of the delicious smell as chocolate soufflés were carried past our table. So I was determined to try the combination myself as soon as possible.'

Serves 6

melted butter, caster sugar and cocoa powder to coat
   the soufflé dishes
250ml full cream milk
20g good-quality cocoa powder
50g good-quality dark chocolate, roughly chopped
1 tablespoon arrowroot, *fécule* (potato flour) or cornflour
3 free range egg yolks
30g caster sugar
6 free range egg whites
a squeeze of lemon juice
icing sugar and cocoa powder for dusting the finished soufflés
pistachio ice-cream, to serve

Brush six 10cm soufflé dishes with melted butter and coat with some caster sugar rolled around the base and sides. Put them in the fridge or freezer to harden. Repeat with more melted butter and a mixture of cocoa powder and sugar in equal amounts. This will ensure a clean and even rise when the soufflés cook. Keep the dishes chilled till needed.

Put the milk in a pan and add the cocoa, pieces of chocolate and arrowroot. Bring to the boil over a medium heat, whisking all the time till the mixture thickens. Remove the pan from the heat.

Put the egg yolks and half the sugar in a bowl and pour the chocolate mixture over them, stirring continuously. Once the mixture is smooth, let it cool a little. Whisk the egg whites with a pinch of salt and a squeeze of lemon. Start at a slow speed, then increase the speed as you add the remaining sugar one teaspoon at a time. Loosen the chocolate mixture by mixing in one tablespoon of the egg white meringue, and then fold the egg white and chocolate mixture together until thoroughly incorporated, with no flecks of egg white remaining.

Divide the mixture evenly between the prepared dishes and cook in a bain-marie in an oven preheated to 220°C/Gas 7 for ten minutes. Before serving, dust with icing sugar and cocoa. Make a hole in the top of each soufflé and drop in a scoop of pistachio ice-cream as you serve them.

PEARS WITH FLORENTINE CREAM

A contemporary version of the Sixties classic, Poires Belle Hélène, which celebrates the successful marriage of pears and chocolate. Boxes of miniature, wafer-thin Florentines are available in good grocer's and supermarkets, but brandy snaps make a good substitute.

Serves 4

100g golden caster sugar
a litre of water
a little lemon juice
a vanilla pod
8 small pears
200ml double or whipping cream
a little vanilla extract
100g small Florentine biscuits or brandy snaps
100g fine dark chocolate

Dissolve the sugar in the water over a low heat and add a few drops of lemon juice and the vanilla pod. Peel the pears, cut them in half, take out the core and drop the fruit into the syrup. With the pan covered, bring the syrup to the boil, then turn down the heat immediately. Let the pears simmer very gently until translucent and tender to the point of a knife. Depending on the ripeness of the fruit this should take about fifteen minutes, but could take longer if the pears are hard. They really must be butter soft if they are to be good.

Let the pears cool in the syrup for a good hour, then lift them out and put them in a shallow dish in the fridge. Whip the cream softly – it shouldn't be too stiff – with a drop or two of vanilla extract. Roughly chop the biscuits, then fold them into the cream.

Break the chocolate into small pieces and place in a small bowl set over a pan of simmering water. When the chocolate has melted, turn off the heat. Remove the pears from the fridge and fill the hollows in each one with Florentine cream. Drizzle the melted chocolate over the fruit, then let them stand in the fridge for twenty minutes to crisp the chocolate. Serve within half an hour.

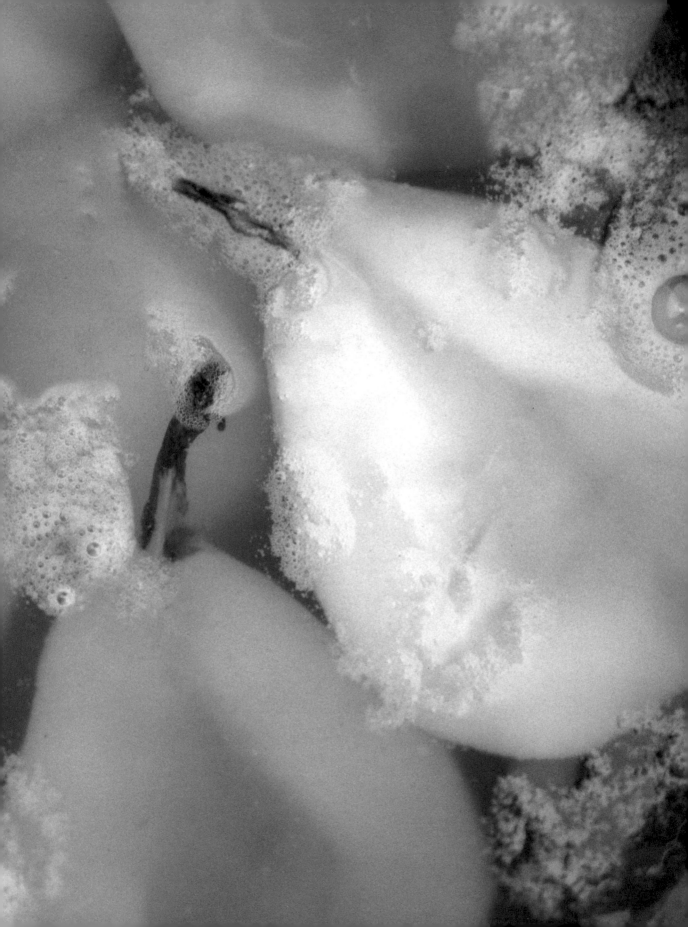

White Chocolate Cardamom Mousse

This gently aromatic mousse is much nicer than it sounds, especially if you use really good white chocolate such as Lindt Vanilla or Valrhona. Don't attempt to make it with anything less – it simply won't work. Serve it in extremely small quantities – no more than an espresso cup per person.

Serves 6–8

8 plump green cardamom pods
100ml milk
3 bay leaves
250g white chocolate
300ml double cream
3 free range egg whites
best-quality cocoa powder for dusting

Break the cardamom pods open and extract the seeds. Crush them lightly, then add them to the milk and bay leaves in a small saucepan. Warm the seasoned milk over a moderate heat until it approaches the boil. Remove from the heat.

Meanwhile, break the chocolate into small pieces and melt in a bowl balanced over a pan of gently simmering water. It is best if the bottom of the bowl does not touch the water. Overheating the chocolate will cause it to go lumpy, so as soon as it starts to melt, turn off the heat but leave the bowl in place.

Whip the cream so that it forms soft mounds rather than peaks. In other words it should not be too stiff. Beat the egg whites to stiff peaks.

When the chocolate is completely melted, remove from the heat and pour the warm milk on to it through a sieve. Stir the chocolate and milk together till velvety.

Scoop the mixture on to the stiffly beaten egg whites and fold gently together with a large metal spoon (a thick wooden one will knock the air out). Now fold into the softly whipped cream.

Scrape into a serving bowl or espresso cups and refrigerate for three or four hours till set. Dust with cocoa or serve with a jug of the chocolate sauce on page 287 or page 288.

CHOCOLATE CAKE

My first-ever piece of cake was one I took home from a party in a paper serviette, its icing sticking to the paper. I have worshipped cake ever since.

Whether you like your chocolate cake mile high or thin and intensely chocolatey, you will find its quality dictated by the type of chocolate you use. For depth of flavour and ease of melting, a fine chocolate with a cocoa butter content above 60 per cent is essential. Add free range eggs, golden unrefined sugar and organically produced flour and you have a head start to the sort of cake that dreams are made of.

I offer two cakes here. One, a rich, quickly made cake with a fudgy centre; the other a nutty refrigerator cake. I have thrown in a handful of those crunchy little cakes made from cornflakes and syrup that most of us will have made when we were young – simply because despite our adoration of the sticky, moist, dark chocolate cake I believe we secretly still like them.

CHOCOLATE ESPRESSO CAKE

When it comes out of the oven the cake should still be moist – sticky even – in the middle. As it cools the cake will sink slightly and the crust will crisp.

On cooling, the outside of the cake becomes sponge-like, whilst the centre remains dense and fudgy.

Serves 8

180g fine dark chocolate, chopped
a small espresso (about 3 tablespoons very strong coffee)
140g butter, diced
5 free range eggs, separated
200g golden caster sugar
1 teaspoon baking powder
2 tablespoons cocoa powder
90g plain flour

Line the base of a 21–23cm shallow springform cake tin with silicone baking parchment, buttering the tin lightly to hold it in place.

Melt the chopped chocolate in a heatproof bowl set over a pan of simmering water. As soon as it starts to soften, add the coffee and leave it for two or three minutes. Stir very gently, then when the chocolate has melted add the butter. Stir until it has melted.

Meanwhile, beat the egg whites with an electric mixer till stiff, then fold in the sugar. Mix the baking powder with the cocoa powder and flour. Remove the chocolate from the heat, quickly stir in the egg yolks, then slowly, firmly and gently fold the melted chocolate into the egg whites. Lastly sift in the flour and cocoa mixture.

Stir the mixture tenderly with a large metal spoon, taking care not to knock out any air. It should feel light and wobbly. Do not overmix – just enough to fold in the flour. Scoop into the lined tin and bake in an oven preheated to 180°C/Gas 4 for thirty-five minutes. Leave to cool in its tin, then turn out.

No-Cook Chocolate Cake

There are many versions of this refrigerator chocolate cake but this is the best. Why? Because it is made with a generous hand, rather than those versions that include cheap chocolate and too many biscuits. You only need a square or two, and an espresso on the side.

Serves 8

340g fine chocolate
200g butter
90g each hazelnuts, almonds and Brazil nuts
2 free range eggs
75g raisins
50g natural-dye glacé cherries
75g digestive biscuits, roughly crumbled

Line a 20cm square cake tin with silicone baking parchment. You can use greaseproof but you may end up picking it off the finished cake bit by bit. Melt 230g of the chocolate and all the butter in a heavy-bottomed saucepan over a moderate heat.

Spread the nuts on a baking sheet or grill pan and toast under a hot grill till the skins start to blister. Rub the nuts with a cloth, discard any of the skins that have flaked off and return the nuts to the grill until they are golden.

Remove the chocolate from the heat when completely melted and stir in most of the toasted nuts (reserve a few for decoration). Beat the eggs lightly with a fork and add to the chocolate and nuts with the raisins and most of the cherries. Stir in the crumbled biscuits, then spoon into the lined cake tin. Leave in the fridge overnight to set.

When the cake is completely set, melt the remaining chocolate in a small bowl set over a pan of simmering water. Pour the chocolate over the cake, then scatter over the reserved nuts and cherries and drizzle with any remaining melted chocolate.

CHOCOLATE CORNFLAKE CAKES

For all the gorgeous chocolate cakes around (and there are many), I still have a soft spot for these crunchy, chewy little cakes. I include them partly because when looking for a recipe for them recently I found it surprisingly difficult to find one. Oh come on, don't tell me you don't like them.

Makes about 15

50g butter
4 tablespoons golden syrup
100g good-quality plain chocolate
75g cornflakes

Gently melt the butter, syrup and chocolate in a small, heavy pan. Stir in the cornflakes. Place large spoonfuls of the mixture on a buttered baking sheet and leave to set in the refrigerator.

INDEX